LOSERS
LIKE US

LOSERS
LIKE US

REDEFINING DISCIPLESHIP
AFTER EPIC FAILURE

DANIEL HOCHHALTER

David C Cook®
transforming lives together

LOSERS LIKE US
Published by David C Cook
4050 Lee Vance View
Colorado Springs, CO 80918 U.S.A.

David C Cook Distribution Canada
55 Woodslee Avenue, Paris, Ontario, Canada N3L 3E5

David C Cook U.K., Kingsway Communications
Eastbourne, East Sussex BN23 6NT, England

The graphic circle C logo is a registered trademark of David C Cook.

Unless otherwise noted, all Scripture quotations are taken from the Holy Bible,
New International Version®, NIV®. Copyright © 1973, 2011 by Biblica, Inc.™
Used by permission of Zondervan. All rights reserved worldwide. www.zondervan.
com. Scripture quotations marked NRSV are taken from the New Revised
Standard Version Bible, copyright 1989, Division of Christian Education of the
National Council of the Churches of Christ in the United States of America.
Used by permission. All rights reserved. Scripture quotations marked NASB
are taken from the New American Standard Bible®, Copyright © 1960, 1995
by The Lockman Foundation. Used by permission. (www.Lockman.org.)

ISBN 978-1-4347-0840-3
eISBN 978-0-7814-1199-8

© 2014 Daniel A. Hochhalter

The Team: Renada Thompson, Nick Lee, Ingrid Beck, Karen Athen
Cover Design: James Herschberger
Cover Photo: Thinkstock

Printed in the United States of America
First Edition 2014

1 2 3 4 5 6 7 8 9 10

061514ls

To the Lents Home Community of
Imago Dei, Portland, Oregon

JOIN THE CONVERSATION

Thank you for reading this book; I hope it encourages you. To learn more about my experiences and my ongoing healing, to get study questions for the book, or to share questions, comments, or your own loser story, find me on Facebook or visit me at www.danielhochhalter .com.

CONTENTS

Foreword 11

Preface 15

Acknowledgments 17

1. An Introduction to Losers—A Personal and Biblical
   History of Infamy 21
2. The Nobodies—Famous for Nothing 35
3. The Zealot—When You Care So Much It Hurts
   (Others) 45
4. The Shadow-Dweller—A Lifetime of Being
   Upstaged 57
5. The Bigot—Admit It, You're One Too 71
6. The Pragmatist—Too Practical to Dream Big 81
7. The Uber-Loser—Hated by Everyone but Jesus 95
8. The Betrayer—Is There a Road to No Return? 109
9. The Doubter—Yeah, Right, When Pigs Fly 123
10. The Egotist—Oh Lord, It's Hard to Be Humble 139
11. The Kid—Who Invited the Pipsqueak? 157
12. The Screwup—When You Just Can't Get It Right . .173
13. The Greatest Loser of All—No One Deserves the
    Title More 195
14. The Kingdom of Losers Like Us—Where Do We Go
    from Here? 211

Notes 231

FOREWORD

Do not put this book down.

Normally I would add, "just trust me," but I won't because you probably don't know me. I am not a scholar. I am not an author. I am not a pastor. I certainly do not hold credentials usually required of people who write forewords to books. I am simply a gal in her thirties who helps lead a home community at Imago Dei in Portland, Oregon, and who has been privileged to walk alongside Dan and his wife, Priscilla, for the past several years. They have become family.

But that is not why I am asking you to read this book.

When Dan told us he was writing a book called *Losers Like Us*, in which he identified with the disciples in their loser traits, I volunteered to be one of the first readers. I knew the book would be well done because Dan is an intelligent man who is not afraid to be honest, and I knew of his hardships and his ongoing healing. But deep down, I expected nothing more than a good read. After all, I definitely did not classify myself as a loser.

This book is for other people, I thought.

Yet as I started reading, I began to see without a doubt that I *was* one of those other people. Like Dan, and the twelve disciples, and even you. We are all losers.

Let that truth sink in for a moment. Yes, I know it's a bit uncomfortable. But believe me—it is the most beautiful place imaginable. It is not something to fear. You will find yourself on every page of this book, and that is a good thing.

You see, this book will simultaneously break you and heal you.

At the start of each chapter, as you begin to read about a particular "loser" disciple, you may be tempted to think, *Yeah, I probably won't relate very much to this one.*

But as you keep reading, your next thought will be, *Uh-oh. That is totally me.*

Followed by, *Dan's right; I am a loser too.* And that is the part that breaks you.

Yet you are not left in brokenness, because Dan always points you back to Christ and how much he loves you. And that is the part that heals you.

Jesus purposely surrounded himself with the very type of person we try to be better than. For me, that is where the real healing took place. As a sometime overachiever, I am tempted to say, "Well, at least I am doing better than…[whomever]." I rely on my own merits to convince myself that I am worthy of God's love. But Dan strips the disciples, and me, to what we really are: a bunch of awkward, messed-up, doubting people whom Jesus found worth dying for. Because Jesus didn't die for the polished version of us—the version we try to present to the world; he died for the real version, the one we don't want to see in the mirror.

Facing a love like that will change your life, and there's nothing to do in response but fall on your knees and say in response, "Thank you. I love you. Here is everything I am. Take it." We see being a loser as something to abhor, but Jesus sees it as something he can love and use.

Now, *that* is healing.

So this is not a traditional study of remote biblical figures, but rather a look at all of us. It is not about how to overcome failure, yet it is about triumph. It is not written from the perspective of one who is healed of brokenness, but instead is written by one who gained heaven's perspective as he wrote it.

That perspective, to me, is the most important characteristic of this book. Because as you read about how Dan wrestles through his story, suddenly you'll realize it is your story too. And the truth of it will open your eyes to a God who uses "upside-down" theology to tell his own love story. He uses the small and weak and foolish—losers—to shame the seemingly great and wise and strong (1 Cor. 1:27–28).

This revelation left me broken of my pride and my tendency to measure myself against an economy of achievement. But simultaneously, it also healed me in the most glorious way possible. Me, the girl who did not even realize her own brokenness, her own need for healing. God's grace can be sneaky like that.

Only Dan could have written this book in all of its gritty honesty. Our home community can attest that Dan has experienced many dark days, trying to find a reason for the pain and loss in his life. And while we don't claim to have all of the answers, we are pretty confident that we know at least one.

You are holding it right now. It is a story that needs to be shared.

Because if this is what a loser is, then I am proud to call myself a loser. I say this boldly and without shame. We are all losers, and we are all in good company. And you will see why.

To God be the glory, forever and ever, amen.

Rebekah Birt, fellow loser

PREFACE

In 2008, after seven years of preparation, I failed my PhD.

It was my final oral examination. I walked into a book-lined office. My two examiners—both strangers to me, as is customary in the British university system—sat at a table, stoic and distant.

Their job was to question me rigorously about my research and my conclusions, as represented in my written dissertation. My job was to give answers that showed convincingly that my work was sound, and worthy of a PhD (in Britain, a DPhil)—the degree for which I had labored.

By their third question, I was in trouble.

Within forty-five minutes, I was done.

In the examiners' final decision, not only did I fail, but also I was not allowed to rewrite and resubmit my work to the university for a second try at the PhD degree.

Ever.

It was over. My dream of a PhD was dead.

You might have lots of questions, as I did. How could this happen? Couldn't I appeal the decision, or transfer at least partial credit to another school, or start all over someplace else? And most of all, since my advisors (one in England and one in the United

States) had approved my work, why did the examiners reject it so decisively?

I've heard all of those questions and more. I've asked them myself, a million times.

But this book is not about that. This book is about what has happened since.

I can't explain exactly how, when, or where everything went so terribly wrong. All I know is, it happened.

And over time, it is radically changing my concept of discipleship.

This book is about that change.

ACKNOWLEDGMENTS

I am an introvert. When life goes sideways, my default is to withdraw inside myself and shut out the world.

Bur during the last few years of crisis as I have felt adrift, metaphorically, on the open sea, I've realized how much I need other people. Now, as I look back, I can see those who have been there with me, whose presence has strengthened and sustained me.

First, I want to thank everyone in the Lents Home Community of Imago Dei—especially its original leaders, Terry (now with Jesus) and Shari Shoman, and its core members who went through the book and the study questions together: Debbie Barnhart, Jared and Bekah Birt, Jeff and Ineke Glavor, Brad and Sara Franklin, Joe and Beyth Greenetz, Mark and Marissa Hunter, Heather Marsh, Kristin Sanger, and Adam and Jocelyn Talbot. Although various others have been part of the group too, you were the ones who studied this book together, and for that I thank you. You welcomed me when I was standoffish and whiny. When you heard my story, you rallied around me in prayer. You didn't offer me annoying advice or formulaic scriptures, promising they would magically remove my pain. Instead, you allowed me to hide, to grieve, and to heal at my own pace. You are a community of true Christ-followers in every way. And because of your support and encouragement, I dedicate this book to you.

Second, for donating time to review and respond to the rough early versions of this manuscript, I want to thank my original readers and consultants: Bekah Birt, Mark Burton, Becca DeWhitt, Rob and Susan Dixon, J. Dale Erbele, and Ken Lawler. I appreciate your honest feedback, your insights, and your friendship.

Third, I want to thank Jenni Burke at D.C. Jacobson & Associates, whose editing and invaluable endorsement drew attention to the proposal; Jeane Wynn at Wynn Wynn Media and Karla Colonnieves at David C Cook for getting the word out about the book; and Ingrid Beck and the rest of the team at David C Cook for their expertise and support. Frankly, I feel like I hit the jackpot with this great company, and I am grateful to them—especially to Renada Thompson, who found my proposal and has believed in this book from the beginning.

Fourth, I want to thank my family for always loving me, even though we are all slightly nuts—in the most adorable way.

Finally, I want to thank my wife and lover, Priscilla. Thanks for your countless hours of editing, proofreading, designing, and so much more. I wish I could have given you security instead of chaos. Yet you became my strength. You've lifted me up when I wanted to "lay down and die." You've believed in me when I haven't believed in myself. I love you.

The righteous man always resembles more a loser than a victor,
for the Lord lets him be tested and assailed to his utmost limits
as gold is tested in a furnace.
Martin Luther

1

AN INTRODUCTION TO LOSERS
A PERSONAL AND BIBLICAL HISTORY OF INFAMY

I've always enjoyed writing, and writing experts say, "Write what you know." So for years, I searched for an area in which I could write with true expertise—but I never found it. Finally, as I began to write my life story, I was forced to acknowledge one topic about which I am truly qualified to write.

The topic? Being a loser.

It took me a long time to realize that I am eminently qualified to discuss "loserness." Not *losing*, mind you, but *being* a loser. I am an expert on the subject.

I actually have proof. Recently I stumbled across an online test called "Are You a Loser?"[1] The test asked questions about my age, the movies I like, how I behave in public, and so on. I scored in the top 10 percent, meaning 90 percent of the populace is cooler than I am.

This gives me pause.

As a kid, I always suspected the "cool" gene had somehow skipped my house, but I honestly thought (or at least hoped) I would fall somewhere in the middle. However, the test is on the Internet, so it must be true.

When I was eleven, my folks divorced. I became a latchkey kid. I flunked sixth grade. I got fat. Just before dating age.

I recovered enough to finish high school and become the first in my family to go to college. I earned a broadcasting degree and became a Christian deejay with my own program, hoping to inspire the masses. But I just wasn't a "radio personality."

I switched to youth ministry, dreaming of revivals that would sweep the nation. But I attracted only a handful of great local kids.

I finished seminary and enrolled in a doctoral program at a British university to pursue the highest degree offered in academia: a doctor of philosophy (DPhil), which Americans call a PhD. After landing a great job as a teacher in a Christian high school, I was able to work toward that degree by staying in the United States during the school year and flying to England for concentrated reading and writing each summer.

Finally, this loser was living his dream.

But in 2008, after seven years of study, I hit a new low in my loser history.

I failed my final examination (oral defense) and lost my PhD.

All that time, all that money—down the drain. Nobody could find a way to salvage one shred of credit or achievement from the wreckage (it's a long story, but believe me, I tried).[2]

How could that be? During all of my research, my experienced British advisor had rigorously critiqued and corrected my work.[3] He kept encouraging me that all of his doctoral students at that university had passed and that I was definitely on track—"in the ballpark."

However, to my examiners, I was not only *not* in the ballpark, but not even on the same *planet* as the ballpark.

I had flamed out.

I returned to the United States and, within weeks, lost my dream job at the Christian high school.

Every crumb of capability I thought I possessed had been violently invalidated—on two continents.

Day after day I lay in bed like a stone, urgently reminding myself to breathe.

I had no career. No prospects. Nothing. And no money or motivation to pursue yet another new direction, even if I had one.

Paralyzed, I stood in the rubble of midlife with nothing to show for my past—or my future—except a slew of false starts. How could I convince potential employers of my worth to them when I couldn't even see any in myself?

In my devastated state, self-accusations dive-bombed me like bats screeching in the night. How could I have blown it so badly? What had made me think I could ever succeed? Had any of my gifts, dreams, or desires ever been worth anything at all? Ever?

Since then, despite encouragement from others, I have continued to battle these demons. In a world that requires skills and credentials I don't have, I am an underachiever.

I am a loser.

But a ray of hope shines through. The ray of hope is in how we define winners and losers, especially losers. Allow me to explain.

We are all losers, really. We live in a broken world. And there is no formula, no simple two-step path to becoming a winner.

This revelation is pretty distasteful, especially in the United States. Due to our famous "can-do" spirit and well-known sense of entitlement, Americans don't even like to admit minor setbacks—unless they are mere lessons learned on the way to victory. We're addicted to winning and success.

Yet there is always someone better right behind us. So eventually, we experience a crash that no amount of effort can overcome. We hit a wall. We fail.

Sooner or later, we all end up on the trash heap. The landscape is littered with yesterday's heroes, each discarded as soon as the next one comes along.

You may be saying, "Then why read this book? I already know I'm a loser; what I really want is *not* to be one."

If that is you, this book won't help. It is not that kind of book.

No, it is a plea to stop the striving, embrace our loserness, and learn to see ourselves through the lens of God's love.

It is about God loving losers. And it is about his odd habit of using the losers of the world to do great things.

So what exactly is a loser? In researching a working definition, I found numerous online dictionaries and discussions that offered multiple definitions of the word. Typical of the Internet, I had to dig through a lot of manure to find a few gems. I'll share a few here and let you decide which is which.

According to the Internet, a loser is…

"[S]omebody who is ugly, has no friends and no life, and nobody likes them."[4] Ouch.

"Someone who gives up on things too quickly without trying … a follower/wannabe … a social outcast … someone that is ignorant and self-centered and does not care about anyone but themselves."[5] A pretty good definition.

"[S]omeone who has never or seldom been successful at a job, personal relationship, etc."[6] I guess "etc" means whatever you want it to mean.

And here is perhaps the best definition of all:

"[Someone] who uses the wrong hand to make the 'L' symbol on her forehead."[7] Perfect!

The word *loser* is used in so many contexts that it has become ambiguous, packed with multiple meanings. So I'll stick with the basics—Losers 101, if you will. In the swirling bog of print and online dictionaries, I have found that the various definitions of the word fall into three major themes: losing in the area of competitiveness, losing in the area of achievements, and losing in the area of social interaction and acceptance.

The first definition, in the context of competition with others, is the most obvious: a loser is one who loses—or, as has been stated, one who does not win. Compared to other definitions, the loser under this definition is the easiest to identify. The one who wins is the winner; everyone else is not.

The second definition is less black-and-white: a loser is one who fails to achieve. Despite his best efforts, this person just can't make it. He may lack skill, luck, or self-awareness. He may grossly overestimate his skills so that he can't see the disaster coming until after it happens, and even then he might blame it on someone or something else. This loser is defined not by losing a single competitive event, but by racking up a long-term pattern of failure.

The final definition of loser is least clear-cut of all because it is based on slippery social values: a loser is one who doesn't "fit in."

Instead, she stands out—and not in a good way. This loser does not meet popular standards of what is normal or desirable. She's "odd"—not enough to call the authorities, but just enough to raise an eyebrow. She may inflict her offbeat interests on hapless others who are desperately trying to squirm out of the conversation.

Obviously, these three arenas—competition, achievement, and sociability—do not represent every possible area of loserness. And even within these categories, the boundaries may overlap or blur. A loser in one context might not be a loser in another.

For example, in the 2007–2008 season of the NFL, after winning every game in the regular season and in the playoffs, the New England Patriots headed to Super Bowl XLII with an awesome 18–0 record. Facing them were the wild-card New York Giants, with a far-from-awesome record of 10–6.

The Patriots were a sure thing, right?

But to everyone's surprise, the Giants won, 17–14.

According to the competitive definition of losers, the Patriots were losers that year. However, whether you love them or hate them, can you really call them *losers*—with an 18–1 total record? They lost only one game, but that was the game that counted.

In a big marathon, only one runner comes in first—but thousands of others finish it. Can you honestly call them *losers*?

In a presidential election, two political parties each send their most qualified candidate to compete in the general election. Two top candidates, out of more than three hundred million American citizens—can you really call the one who doesn't win a *loser*?

The label of loser is also relative in the second category: achievements. Is it a greater achievement to get a date with the prettiest cheerleader in school, score a full-ride athletic scholarship to a great university, or win a national science competition? Is it greater to lead a Fortune 500 company or to volunteer at a soup kitchen? Earning a raise or landing a promotion can be considered an achievement. So can winning a video game. So can burping the alphabet. Yet being a "winner" at some of those things might be considered being a "loser" in certain circles.

Socially, the definition is just as ambiguous. Why is a social misfit considered a misfit? An introverted boy who spends all his time reading and then creates an imaginary universe might be considered strange. Yet if one such boy hadn't discovered Beatrix Potter's Peter Rabbit stories and then created his own unique fantasy world, we would not have C. S. Lewis's *Chronicles of Narnia* today.

What is normal? Who decides? As we've seen, the stereotypical definitions of a loser include a non-winner, an underachiever, and a social reject, and one or more of these definitions will apply to all of us in our lifetimes. Even winners don't stay winners forever. At some point, we all will be losers.

My purpose, however, is not to help losers become winners. This is not a self-help book. I've already stated that I will present no magic formulas, no easy principles guaranteeing your entrance into the winner's circle. I can't make you a winner. In all honesty, after decades of trying, I have realized that I can't make myself one either. In fact, I'm done trying.

So, then, what *is* the purpose of this book?

It is to affirm that God loves losers—and he uses them. This is true not only *if and when* they become winners, but *in the midst of* their loserness.

Why is this message needed?

One reason is that when Christians say that God loves you and has a wonderful plan for your life, the unspoken implication is that his "wonderful plan" will make everything in your life better: your job, your status, your health, your character, even your scintillating party persona. Of course most Christians, with the exception of some prosperity theologians, don't promise this outright. But it is often assumed by immature Christians and uncorrected by mature ones.

However, for many of us, the reality is just the opposite. Even as Christians, we still struggle. Once we identify ourselves as Christians, if we still struggle we are often judged by other Christians who think we should know better by now. So, since we can't admit our problems to other Christians, we cry alone to the ceiling: *Where is this wonderful plan for my life? Where is the abundance Jesus promised? Why is screwing up the only thing I do well?*

But "good" Christians aren't supposed to ask questions like that; "good" Christians aren't supposed to feel like failures. I know I have value, the cliché goes, because "God don't make no junk." Yet looking at the mess of our lives, we question the truth of that claim. We fret over our glaring flaws and subpar talents and honestly conclude that we have nothing to offer and therefore God can't use us. Soon, we hesitate to try again for fear of even more failure. Each flop increases our pain and decreases our willingness to risk greater things.

And after getting slapped down a few times by other Christians for experiencing the forbidden feelings of doubt and discouragement, we know better than to share such things again. So we go to church wearing masks of joyful faith, pretending all is well when deep down we know it is not. Thus isolated, we become convinced we are the only ones caught in this struggle. We are certain that when others look in the mirror they see mature servants of Christ who, though imperfect, *really* believe that God doesn't make junk.

On the other hand, when we ourselves look in the mirror, junk is the only thing we see.

Sermons attempt to encourage losers by claiming that in the kingdom, no task is insignificant; every job is a ministry—even washing dishes or weeding the grass. This is true, but we are human; we long to be a part of something that feels significant *to us.* Yet we feel like losers—unskilled, unqualified, and unusable.

But here's the mystery: God loves that face in the mirror, that loser staring back at me. He loves losers—and he uses the unusable.

True, there is no Bible verse saying that if you are a loser, God loves you and prefers to work with you. You won't find that message stated explicitly in any book of Scripture, nor in any great theological commentaries of the past or present.

But you will find it in the lives of the people of the Bible. You will find it in their stories.

I am not talking about the sanitized Sunday school versions of those stories, in which Bible characters are presented as one-dimensional superhumans, bronzed and chiseled like Charlton Heston in *The Ten Commandments*, with their faces gazing longingly up at the heavens. In these portrayals, the Bible heroes never commit any mistakes or sins—or, if they do, they quickly and completely turn from the error of their ways with pious prayers of repentance. Their questions and statements are interpreted not as indicative of the ignorance or arrogance of flawed human beings, but only of their desire for deeper holiness.

After all, Old Testament heroes saw miracles defy natural law, and spoke with God face-to-face—so how could they continue to exhibit any sin? And New Testament heroes walked with Jesus himself, following in his very footsteps and imitating his very acts—so how could they continue in any imperfection?

When we lift up these spiritual giants as, well, spiritual giants, we begin to believe that they are examples of how God changes unclean humans into a new, improved super-race to fulfill his commands—immediately, successfully, and without any trace of doubt or fear. That could be us, we believe, *if* we let God change us. So we pray that God will change us; yet we still feel just as incapable as before. We will never be like them, we tell ourselves. We are not even close.

Yet once the stereotypes are removed from the biblical characters and their stories, all that remains is a bunch of sinful, imperfect people. Take away the temptation to shoehorn them into models of perfect holiness, and what's left? Humans. Dress them in their humanity, and you have a bunch of failures. People with patchy, mediocre résumés. People who are fallen and broken.

Losers.

I find it interesting that Scripture never hides the flaws of the people in God's story. Instead, their faults, mistakes, and sins are preserved in the world's best-selling book for all to read. It is only in relatively recent interpretations, made thousands of years after the fact, that we have given them superhero status.

When I taught high school Bible classes, I once mentioned the topic of losers in the Bible to another Bible teacher. He replied, "You mean, Saul and Jezebel and the Pharisees and—"

"No," I said, "I mean Moses and David and Peter." These heroes of faith were human, like us: longing for perfection but perpetually, daily, coming up short. I am not sure why we shrink from seeing them as flawed, sinful, and dysfunctional. Perhaps we think it is a sacrilege to do so. Since God is perfect, we assume that those he has used to do great things must be perfect too.

Yet this is what makes the story so exciting. God's choice *is* perfect. Those he has chosen to do kingdom work *are* the perfect ones to do it. And yet, they are always flawed individuals. Losers. This pattern, consistent throughout Scripture, is a remarkable testament to God's creativity and grace: he chooses ordinary, broken humans to introduce his mercy and love to an ordinary, broken world.

Now it begins to make sense to me. If God had used "winners"—the most beautiful, wealthy, successful, and powerful among us—to speak grace and encouragement to those who feel average and insignificant, the message just wouldn't sink in. All of us losers would think, *You're such a winner that I can't even relate to you! Even if I do follow Jesus, I'll still never be like you.*

No, to a loser, the testimony of another loser is much more helpful. And the Bible is packed full of these testimonies, of losers who sincerely want to follow God but whose quirks and sins get in the way. Except for the Holy Trinity, every character in the Bible is a failure—a loser. Yet as an illustration of God's grace, God's work is completed through them nonetheless.

This pattern is visible throughout the scriptural stories, and even beyond them to the present day. Last time I checked, God's story is not over yet. The book of Revelation has not yet been completely fulfilled. The pattern of God loving and using losers continues to be written through us today.

But there are far too many losers in the Bible to cover in one book. So I have chosen to reflect on the group whom Jesus called to be his closest associates and trainees—the ones we call the twelve disciples.[8] In Scripture (Matt. 10:2–4; Mark 3:16–19; and Luke 6:12–16), they are listed as follows:

- Simon, whom Jesus renamed Peter, meaning "the rock" (Matt. 16:18)—a fisherman by trade (Matt. 4:18)
- Andrew, a fisherman and brother of Simon Peter (Mark 1:16), and a follower of John the Baptist before meeting Jesus (John 1:40)
- James, a fisherman and son of Zebedee (Matt. 4:21)
- John, a fisherman and son of Zebedee also (Mark 1:19)—Jesus's nickname for the brothers James and John was "sons of thunder" (Mark 3:17)
- Philip, from Bethsaida, like Peter and Andrew (John 1:44)
- Bartholomew, also called Nathanael, a friend of Philip (John 1:45)
- Thomas, also called Didymus (John 21:2), which means "the twin"
- Matthew the tax collector (Matt. 9:9), also called Levi son of Alphaeus (Mark 2:14)
- James, son of Alphaeus (Luke 6:15—if this is the same Alphaeus as Matthew's father, then this James would be Matthew's brother, but the relationship is not known for certain), also sometimes called James the Less
- Simon the Zealot (Luke 6:15), a member of the radical Jewish nationalist movement called Zealots

- Judas Thaddaeus, also called Judas son of James
  (or, in some versions of Matthew 10:3, Lebbaeus
  Thaddaeus)
- Judas the betrayer of Jesus, called Judas Iscariot
  (Luke 6:16) to distinguish him from the other
  Judas

Note that in making his selection, Jesus bypassed the religious institutions and took it to the streets. He snubbed the head of the class, the cream of the crop. He ignored credentials, achievements, and the "who's who" of religious piety. He jettisoned every qualification we deem important in leadership and chose instead to call ordinary people—mostly manual laborers with little or no education, ministry experience, or leadership skills.

They didn't bring much to the table.

They certainly were nothing to write home about.

And I haven't even listed their alarming personality flaws yet.

Yet, on the night before Jesus chose his disciples, he spent the night praying (Luke 6:12–16).

So, if he prayed before choosing them, why did he end up choosing such losers? Either Jesus's prayer was not answered, or the disciples he chose were God's own choice—weaknesses, sins, flaws, and all.

I am pretty sure it is not the former.

Even more amazing, these twelve didn't suddenly morph into superheroes the moment they were called; instead, they stumbled after Jesus, hobbled by faults and sins, constantly jockeying for "Disciple of the Year" and missing the whole point.

They were clueless and self-centered, imperfect and flawed.

They were losers in the eyes of the world.

They were *us*.

Yet after three intimate years with Jesus—traveling with him, ministering with him, seeing his miracles and hearing his teachings—they became the powerful foundation on which he established the body of Christ on earth, now over a billion strong.

The chapters that follow are not impersonal studies but rather a series of personalized reflections, comparing my life to the lives of the first twelve Christ-followers. When I hold them up to my own life like a mirror, I am encouraged to see that their stories, like mine, are filled with paralyzing faults and sins—yet they were greatly used by God.

If God can use these losers, even in spite of themselves, then he can use you and me.

2

THE NOBODIES

FAMOUS FOR NOTHING

Imagine you are an up-and-coming actor, auditioning to play one of the twelve disciples in the next major epic by a world-renowned director. Which role would you shoot for?

Peter, surely the most famous of the Twelve? His part would have lots of screen time and lots of meaty lines.

Or Thomas, who famously doubted and then believed in Jesus's resurrection?

Or the complicated role of Judas Iscariot?

You're certain that any of the twelve roles will be exciting. So you try out.

When the casting is posted, you scan the list and are thrilled to see that you have a part: James, the son of Alphaeus.

"Yes!" you say, half to yourself. "James was one of the top three disciples—as in Peter, James, and John!"

But a fellow cast member overhears and says, "You're thinking of the wrong James; you're thinking of James and John, the sons of Zebedee. This is not *that* James; this is the *other* James."

"The *other* James? You mean James the brother of Jesus?"

"Well," your new friend continues, "Jesus did have a brother named James, but many believe he was never a disciple. This is a *third* James—the *other* other James."

"You mean there are multiple people named James in the New Testament, and *two* of them are disciples?"

"Correct."

Okay, you think to yourself, *this should still be a good part. It's still a disciple, right?* So you race to your Bible to research this *other* other James, the son of Alphaeus.

But the more you look, the more your shoulders sag. *This* James sure isn't a major part. He's not even a bit part. In Scripture, he doesn't have a single line. In most scenes, he'll probably be in the background, providing obscure, exaggerated expressions in response to the action taking place elsewhere.

In fact, this James is so insignificant in Scripture that Bible scholars call him "James the Less."

You sigh, realizing the only distinction this disciple can claim is that without him, Jesus would have had only eleven disciples.

This *other* other James is mentioned just four times in the New Testament (Matt. 10:3; Mark 3:18; Luke 6:15; Acts 1:13)—and each time it is by name only, as part of the roster of the twelve disciples. There is no context or backstory about him. What skills did he bring to the work of the disciples? How did he relate to them? How did he participate in Jesus's ministry? How did he interact with Jesus?

Of course, being an actor, you tactfully ask the director why he cast you in this small role, couching your displeasure in respectful tones while dropping subtle pleas for at least a speaking part.

The director gets the hint and offers to recast you. You thank him and jump at the chance.

He offers you the part of Thaddeus.

Thaddeus? Who on earth is Thaddeus?

Again, you rush to your Bible to do your character study.

And again, your heart sinks.

Like James the son of Alphaeus, Thaddaeus is mentioned in the same four lists of disciples. But unlike James, he has two names: Thaddaeus in Matthew 10:3 and Mark 3:18; and Judas son of James in Luke 6:16 and Acts 1:13. At least he has one speaking line, a single question during the Last Supper.

You sigh in defeat. For this major motion picture, you're stuck with a miniscule part.

No matter how you spin it, your role in this grand drama seems tiny and insignificant. In a world that celebrates star power, you're little more than a warm body on the set, an anonymous face in the crowd.

If I had been cast in the exciting story of Jesus's life but my part was that of either Thaddaeus or James the son of Alphaeus, I would have been greatly disappointed. Sure, I would have played the part, but with the attitude of a wet cat: sulky and irritated.

As a drama instructor and a lifelong lover of acting and directing, I'm drawn to the spotlight. I've never been intimidated by being onstage in front of an audience; in fact, I enjoy the thrill and excitement. Yes, I get butterflies. That's part of the rush. But I still love to get attention, any way I can.

I don't think this is a pathological need. I think I just enjoy it.

Loving the spotlight, in and of itself, is not a sin. Some people hate to be in the spotlight; others like it. I am in the latter group. So to me, being cast in a minor, marginal role would be torture.

Yet I wonder, in real life, if that is the role I am destined to play. No matter how hard I've tried, no matter what preparations I've made, the spotlight has always eluded me. The harder I chase it, the more it escapes me, like a car speeding away in the night. At some point, while chasing the fleeing car, I trip and skid across the pavement. With sweat and blood running down my forehead, it dawns on me that I might never catch it.

And as its taillights disappear in the distance, I am forced to reexamine exactly why I am pursuing it.

In the movie *Indiana Jones and the Last Crusade*, as Indiana passionately chases after the Holy Grail from which Christ drank at the Last Supper, his father pointedly asks him, "Do you seek the cup for *his* glory, or yours?"

The question hits a mark in me as well.

My problem is typical among spotlight lovers: somewhere along the way, many of us move from seeing the spotlight as a fun but neutral part of life, to seeing it as the *goal* of life. Instead of using the spotlight to reveal Jesus to others, we use Jesus as a spotlight to draw attention to ourselves. I don't have hard statistics, but I suspect the majority of us have subconsciously shifted the focus this way at one time or another, whether we admit it or not.

But God doesn't call everyone to be in the spotlight. He needs both "big names" and understudies, leading ladies and bit players, heroes and extras.

In many ways, it is easier to relate to the "big name" disciples. They appear as active participants in many of the gospel stories. Their characters are more developed. Their personalities are more visible. In Scripture, they interact directly with Jesus, respond to his challenges, and react to his miracles. Because they appear so frequently throughout the New Testament, there are more opportunities to learn about them. They are the major players.

However, in a strange twist, it is their very dominance in Scripture that makes them seem less approachable to me.

I think most people see themselves as unqualified to join Jesus's inner circle with Peter, James, and John. Even today, most people are less likely to relate to megachurch pastors, nationally or internationally known preachers, or world-famous theologians than to an insignificant nobody—someone like James son of Alphaeus, who never speaks in Scripture, or Thaddaeus, who throws out one question during the Last Supper that could have been asked by anyone: "Lord, why do you intend to show yourself to us and not to the world?" (John 14:22). That's all we know about these two disciples. Everything else is speculation and interpretation.

Scripture mentions several people named James, and we don't know if this James is the same as one or more of them, or different from all of them.

Could this James, the disciple, be a brother of Levi the tax collector, also called Matthew, who, like James, is listed as the "son of Alphaeus" (Mark 2:14)? Or could this James be the same person as Jesus's brother James, who may or may not have been the same person as "James the younger," son of Mary (Mark 15:40), in which case perhaps Mary outlived Joseph and had a second husband, named Alphaeus? Or perhaps this Mary is a *different* Mary—not Jesus's mother?

Is your head spinning?

Similarly, we know little about Thaddaeus, also called Judas, except that he is not Judas Iscariot (John 14:22) but rather is "Judas son of James" (Luke 6:16 and Acts 1:13). Of course, James is a common name, so again, *which* James? James the brother of Jesus? If yes, then is Judas the nephew of Jesus? Or is this James the "*other* other James"? If so, then Thaddaeus and that James might be related, perhaps as father and son. Of course, if James son of Alphaeus is also Mary's son, then Thaddaeus could be Jesus's nephew as well.

Now *my* head is spinning.

The second thing we know about Thaddaeus is that when the disciples are listed, he is always listed next to Simon the Zealot. Could this mean that these two were friends? Relatives? Comrades in the Zealot party? We really don't know.

Some people think Judas Thaddaeus may have written the book of Jude in the New Testament, although not all scholars agree.

How can we discuss individuals about whom we know very little, except for their appearance in a list of names? And since we know nothing about them, is it fair to label them as losers?

But *this* James and *this* Judas (even their names are not unique!) qualify as losers because of their failure to do anything worth recording in Scripture. Even in a tiny pool of only twelve people, they never distinguish themselves. In fact, the Gospels mention them so rarely that we can't even be sure when they were present and when they were not.

Perhaps they stayed in the wings by choice, quietly soaking up everything Jesus said and did. Or perhaps they just lacked the "big personality" to force their way into the story.

I find the former theory difficult to swallow. If they were quietly absorbing Jesus's teaching and putting it into practice, I think sooner or later they would have said or done something interesting enough to be noted in the Gospels. No, I think this James and Thaddaeus represent the faceless masses—those whose lives, skills, and talents are less than stellar, relegating them to seemingly passive roles in Jesus's ministry.

Why did these two disciples, working side by side with other disciples who had many more "speaking parts," fail to attract attention? Did they lack skill, talent, or ambition? Were they shy, fearful, or insecure? Perhaps they withered in the spotlight of Peter's charisma, Simon's zeal, or John's intimacy with Jesus.

I believe they suffered from a fatal case of ordinariness.

Why, then, did Jesus pick them to be his disciples, the foundation of the early church? What could they possibly contribute to the beginning of Christianity if they made no impression on the authors of the Gospels?

These are the same questions I have thrown at the ceiling during many sleepless nights. There are so many people who are funnier, smarter, and more talented than I. What could I possibly do in God's kingdom that someone else can't do better? Why would Jesus call *me* to be his disciple?

But Jesus called James and Thaddaeus for the same reason he called me. He wanted relationship. Whatever it was he saw in them, he needed them. Remember, Jesus prayed all night before choosing his disciples—and when he chose them, James and Thaddaeus were included.

Why?

We'll never know. Maybe even they didn't know.

But Jesus needed them.

And they answered his call.

Being a disciple doesn't start with what we can bring to Jesus, but who we are in Jesus. This is the lesson of James and Thaddaeus.

The Bible is packed with stories about people of faith who did great things; we read about them and long to imitate them. But the Bible reminds us, throughout the Old and New Testaments, that most of the real work is done by countless heroes who remain forever unsung.

Take Elijah, for instance. In 1 Kings 18, he summons fire from heaven to consume a sacrifice to Yahweh before 850 false prophets, right on cue. (Now *that* would be awesome!) Yet the Bible says that at least a hundred other prophets of God were hidden in caves to avoid being slaughtered by Jezebel (1 Kings 18:4). Unlike Elijah, these prophets are not named in Scripture; the spotlight eluded them too. But their work was so important that Jezebel was determined to put an end to it.

Similarly, Luke tells of seventy-two nameless followers of Jesus who, sent by him into the towns ahead of him, were so powerful in the Lord that they returned to Jesus saying, "Even the demons submit to us in your name" (Luke 10:17). And Acts tells of more anonymous followers, scattered throughout Judea and Samaria, who "preached the word wherever they went" (Acts 8:4).

A final example is found in the book of 1 Peter—a letter of encouragement to all Christians throughout the known world at that time, who were suffering violent persecution under Emperor Nero. This letter instructs them on how to testify about Jesus to unbelievers.

Given the fact that Christianity is now known around the world, I would say these unnamed Christians were pretty effective witnesses.

Fame eluded them all, thousands of them. But were it not for them, Christianity most likely would have remained a small, local religion. Their work was critical in the building of the kingdom of God.

In the Bible, unknown disciples far outnumbered the superstars, and the ratio is similar today. So, for all of us modern unknowns, the *other* other James and Judas Thaddaeus are great role models. If you go strictly by the number of appearances, they are failures as disciples. It seems Jesus could have done his ministry just as well without them.

Jesus, however, isn't limited to working solely with those in the spotlight. Though famous speakers and evangelists today can reach thousands of people with one telecast, discipleship is done one relationship at a time by those we will never read about. Their legacy is seen in the lives of those they touched.

James son of Alphaeus and Thaddaeus may appear irrelevant and insignificant, disappearing like two drops of water in an enormous sea.

Two drops of water is not enough for a swim, a bath, or even a drink.

But millions and millions of drops, all combined together, can flood a city, a state, or even a nation.

Perhaps I will never find the spotlight. But my value to the kingdom of God is not determined by my ability to attract or hold the spotlight. Instead, it is determined by my willingness to listen, learn, and be used by Jesus, whenever and however he desires.

This James and Thaddaeus—the nobodies—are still teaching me this lesson, two thousand years after their deaths.

3

THE ZEALOT

WHEN YOU CARE SO MUCH
IT HURTS (OTHERS)

I have an alter ego.

Normally, I am cleverly disguised as a mild-mannered introvert, hidden behind wire-rimmed glasses and a timid expression. I may appear harmless and unobtrusive. However, should some poor sap inadvertently put one toe over the line and touch one of my many hot buttons, I immediately morph into something out of a Japanese horror flick. I call it "Monster Zeal."

This happens very quickly, before anyone can react. And it is not pretty.

I become a spitting cobra.

My tongue flickers violently. My fangs shoot streams of stinging venom, disabling my prey into stunned silence. Only after Monster Zeal detects high levels of discomfort, with my victim making awkward attempts to change the subject or flee the scene, do I finally change back into my quiet, unassuming self.

I never remember exactly what was said during Monster Zeal's appearance. I just know I feel very icky when I become human again.

I'd love to believe my zeal has great potential for good, like the zeal of Martin Luther King Jr., Teddy Roosevelt, or Joan of Arc. But in reality, I think my zeal is more like that of my ten-pound miniature dachshund, Misty: at the first sign of a perceived threat, this sweet, good-natured wiener dog folds back her ears, bares her teeth, lunges forward, and launches a relentless, ear-splitting squeal that sounds as though someone is beating her to death. In all the excitement, she occasionally forgets exactly what she's barking at, but that is irrelevant. The strategy is to bark, continuously and maniacally, until the perceived threat is soundly trounced and driven away—undoubtedly more annoyed than intimidated. My zeal is more like Misty's than Martin Luther King's. Not the way to get into the history books.

This zealous alter ego first began to emerge in eighth grade. In class discussions, I would raise my hand to put in my two cents' worth. Usually, my point was easily shot down, and I quickly learned that starting a debate with "My dad says…" was rhetorically unwise. However, to deflect embarrassment, I'd mutter something sarcastic under my breath and give up the argument.

I remember vowing at that age never to lose a debate again. At first I wasn't sure how I would accomplish this, but by high school I had fine-tuned a technique that seemed to work: if I ever began to feel that I couldn't win a point, I would just look at my opponent and stop talking.

You are probably wishing more people, especially politicians, would try it.

The problem with this strategy, however, was that if I disagreed but stayed silent, there was no outlet for the emotions that sometimes built up inside me. Only after making certain that I could land a couple of zingers would I finally speak up, but I was so unsure of myself that I felt I had to use enough force to verbally knock the other party into a completely different discussion.

Those zingers had a bite. My goal was not just to point out contradictions in logic, but to point out how stupid the other person was for having the audacity to oppose my view. Logic was not my weapon of choice. I preferred sarcasm.

My first published article appeared on the opinion page of our high school newspaper during my sophomore year. A speaker had addressed the student body in an assembly over a controversial issue, and I wrote a response. I was so irritated by this speaker that I bypassed the issue and went straight for the jugular. As far as I was concerned, she wasn't just illogical; she was stupid. My entire opinion piece consisted of clever little slams about how the speaker was "dumber than a kneepad" and "had an IQ a grade lower than bean dip." That was it. That was my rhetorical strategy.

Of course, my strategy overlooked the pesky idea that discussions are about learning from each other, testing personal theories, and maturing one's opinions. With me, it was not about point and counterpoint, listening and learning. It was about crushing the opposition.

Decades later, I am somewhat more mature. I have developed a belief system, personal opinions, and political viewpoints. Issues matter, and outcomes are important. Unfortunately, my strategy of landing zingers has remained with me, and I've gotten better at it. I often see the world as black-and-white, and those who disagree with me as just plain stupid.

I don't discuss issues with people; I launch. What's worse, sometimes I even assume that I know where people stand on an issue based on what they have said about other issues, or on even flimsier presumptions, so I end up going after them for beliefs they may not hold at all. Even if my point is valid, I make things so tense and awkward that people want to squirm out of the conversation.

When I cool off, I can only shake my head and wonder how I got so out of control. After one of these episodes, I felt so guilty that the next day I had to ask a coworker, "At what point did I become a jerk?"

I have difficulty seeing my zealous streak as a good thing. I get irritable during elections. I shout insults at the talking heads on TV. Even during social gatherings or games, my playful trash talk with friends often crosses the line into sensitive territory. I never know I've overstepped until after someone's feelings get hurt. Therefore, in group settings, staff discussions, or committee meetings, I try to keep silent to avoid wounding others. And in the process, I begin to believe that my zeal is yet another nasty trait that must be conquered before God can use me. How could I ever serve in the kingdom of God when most of my energy is spent trying to lasso the flashing hooves and teeth of my dangerous wild-horse passions?

In Jesus's group of disciples, there was at least one who was so zealous that his zeal was actually referenced in his name: Simon the Zealot.

This name may have implied a personality trait, but it was also a political affiliation. Simon was a member of the Zealot party. And joining the Zealots was far more than an indication of how one might vote.

The Zealots espoused an extreme blend of fanatical political and religious beliefs. They carried out and celebrated murderous attacks against the Romans, as well as against any Jews who collaborated or sympathized with Rome.

They were the Al-Qaeda of their day.

As a political organization, the group lasted roughly seventy years. Inspired by the Maccabean revolt against Antiochus Epiphanes IV from 167 to 160 BC, the Zealots rose up around the time of Christ to aggressively oppose Herod the Great—the Jewish "puppet king" installed by Rome. To the Zealots, it was an abomination to live under foreign rule in their God-given promised land. They felt their land should be ruled solely by the laws and authority of Yahweh. Rome, and anyone associated with it, was considered an enemy—not just of the Jews, but of Yahweh.

Shortly after Jesus's birth—which many historians believe took place around 6 BC—the Zealots, led by Judas of Galilee, launched an open rebellion against Rome. At that time, the Zealot party was so violent that it included a class of specially appointed assassins called *Sicarii*, which in Greek means "dagger men." These men patrolled the city with daggers hidden in their sleeves, assassinating both Roman leaders and any Jews they considered sellouts to Rome. The Zealots were involved in the 66 AD revolt, which eventually contributed to the destruction of the temple in 70 AD, and in the 73 AD siege of the fortress at Masada, where nine hundred of them chose suicide over surrender to Rome.

Doctrinally, the Zealots closely resembled the Pharisees. They believed that Yahweh was one God and that Israel should serve only him (Deut. 6:4). They believed in living righteously before him in strict obedience to the Torah and the Prophets.

Such beliefs are admirable. However, human nature being what it is, the Zealots easily transitioned from those beliefs to the belief that *they* were the only true followers of Yahweh, the only ones capable of restoring righteousness and reclaiming their society from pagan Rome. The thinking went like this: "We follow Yahweh, so we are righteous. Rome and its sympathizers do not, so they are evil. Therefore, we have divine license to do whatever it takes to stop that evil, including murder."

They sincerely believed they were pleasing God, even as their victims' blood dripped from their dagger blades. Fanatical and militant, like all revolutionaries they saw only two possible outcomes: victory or death.

This was the world of Simon the Zealot. Like Jesus's other choices, the choice of Simon as a disciple doesn't make much sense.

Jesus preached, "Blessed are the poor in spirit ... the merciful ... the peacemakers" (Matt. 5:3, 7, 9). How could he choose a member of a violent extremist group to follow him?

Perhaps Simon was merely a hanger-on, agreeing with the Zealots' beliefs but not with their violent methods. Maybe he was a Zealot in lip service only, a mere back-room apologist. After all, the cause of championing a return to righteousness was a just one. Could this be what Jesus saw in Simon? If so, perhaps Simon's zeal was not in conflict with Jesus's teachings on a peaceable, holy life.

But we don't know for sure how radical Simon might have been. Remember, he *identified* with the Zealots—so much so that "Zealot" became part of his name. I doubt he earned that label by tacitly supporting their beliefs from a safe distance or by tossing out a few timid comments in a street-corner debate. No, his involvement must've gone much deeper than that.

We have to see Simon for what he really was. He was a Zealot.

That meant he opposed Rome with a vengeance. And, being a true Zealot, it is not unlikely that he had committed violence—even murder—for the cause. Today, he might be called a terrorist.

Yet Jesus called him to be a disciple—an intimate follower of the Prince of Peace. Simon's life path went against everything Jesus taught about the kingdom of God. So why would Jesus choose him? Surely choosing Simon meant trouble. He could have been a fugitive, wanted by Roman authorities because of his suspected actions or associations. He must have been astonished—perhaps even enraged—when Jesus commended the faith of a centurion who was not only a Gentile but also a hated Roman, and a military leader at that (Matt. 8:8–11).

When Simon first heard Jesus speaking about the kingdom of God, he must have experienced a thrill that the day of liberation from the oppressors had finally arrived, quickly followed by a letdown as Jesus described God's new kingdom as a kingdom of peace. Clearly, Simon and Jesus had very different ways of defining the "kingdom of God." All of the disciples seemed to hope and expect that Jesus would establish a physical, political kingdom, but I believe Simon's hopes and expectations were the most fervent and intense of all.

Imagine Jesus teaching the masses to "love your enemies and pray for those who persecute you" (Matt. 5:44) while Simon, eyeing a Roman soldier nearby, caresses the handle of a dagger under his cloak.

Imagine Jesus instructing his disciples to "forgive other people when they sin against you" (Matt. 6:14) as they pass some Jewish tax collectors, famous for extorting illegal taxes from their fellow Jews while their Roman bosses looked the other way. Even worse, Jesus actually *called* a dreaded tax collector, Matthew, to be a disciple with Simon. Scripture doesn't mention Simon's feelings on that subject, but I suspect the interaction between Simon and Matthew sometimes got a bit rough and Jesus had to step between them.

Imagine two of Jesus's disciples mixing it up over politics.

Indeed, Simon the Zealot could have been nothing but trouble. But he chose to follow Jesus anyway.

We've already discussed what might have attracted Jesus to Simon—but conversely, I've also wondered what attracted Simon to Jesus. What possessed a warmonger to follow the upside-down teachings of the Prince of Peace? The two men's theologies, politics, and methodologies were complete opposites. Yet Jesus had something that made Simon want to turn around and follow him. I wonder what that was.

Perhaps it was zeal. Both Simon and Jesus had great zeal. Both operated on the radical fringe of society. Both worked toward a dramatic upheaval of the entire system. And Jesus had no intention of leaving this earth without accomplishing that end—in his time, his way.

But Jesus's zeal was different from Simon's.

Jesus's zeal drew multitudes of the weak, not the strong, and changed hearts not with force but with compassion.

Jesus's zeal produced physical miracles, as when he healed the sick, raised the dead, and calmed the sea (Matt. 8:26; 11:5).

Jesus's zeal was so truthful and convicting that the hard-hearted resisted it with violence, as when the crowds perceived that he was making a claim of deity and tried to stone him (John 8:58–59).

Jesus's zeal pierced the religious hypocrites, not with daggers, but with epithets like "whitewashed tombs" and "vipers" (Matt. 23:27,

33) and with actions like overturning the money changers' tables in the temple:

> When it was almost time for the Jewish Passover, Jesus went up to Jerusalem. In the temple courts he found people selling cattle, sheep and doves, and others sitting at tables exchanging money. So he made a whip out of cords, and drove all from the temple courts, both sheep and cattle; he scattered the coins of the money changers and overturned their tables. To those who sold doves he said, "Get these out of here! Stop turning my Father's house into a market!" His disciples remembered that it is written: "Zeal for your house will consume me." (John 2:13–17)

Zeal is a magnet, and Simon was clearly attracted to this zealous teacher.

The Zealots wanted to free the Jews from the rule of foreign oppressors and establish a theocracy, ruled by Yahweh. Jesus's teachings on the kingdom of God seemed to be a blueprint for the very same thing. Simon must have understood that blueprint to mean the overthrow of Rome—a movement Simon surely would want to join. He didn't quite understand Jesus's goals, but he also couldn't ignore the signs that change was coming. In the end, of course, Jesus was ushering in a kingdom far greater than even Simon could imagine.

I find it intriguing that Jesus chose Simon, the political fanatic, as a disciple apparently without requiring him to change political parties. I think Jesus saw Simon's fanatical zeal as an asset, something that could be used to further God's kingdom.

How can that be? I can hardly imagine Jesus using even my own zeal, which deploys sarcasm and mockery to disparage those whose viewpoints run counter to mine; so how could he possibly use Simon's zeal, which espoused not only mockery but murder?

What exactly is zeal? And is it good or bad?

Most dictionaries define zeal as fervor or enthusiasm, either for something or against something. On one hand, Paul says that we are to never be lacking in zeal to serve the Lord (Rom. 12:11). On the other hand, Paul describes his zeal in persecuting the church before he turned to God (Phil. 3:6), which was clearly not a good thing. But zeal can't be all bad, because it is an attribute of God as well, either in a context of wrath and judgment (Ezek. 36:5; 38:19) or in a context of accomplishment and protection (Isa. 26:11; 37:32).

There are many ways to look at zeal. First, the positive value of zeal is in the eye of the beholder. As an example, compare Rush Limbaugh and Michael Moore: both are zealous, but depending on your political views you might find one inspiring and well considered, and the other repulsive and idiotic. You wonder why the entire nation does not rally around your favorite zealot, while being horrified that people even listen to the sewage put forth by the other. So, clearly, if I disagree with someone and call him zealous, it's not a compliment; but if I agree with him, it is.

Second, zeal itself is amoral—neither good nor bad. Only the resulting actions are good or bad. For example, compare Hitler and Gandhi—again, both extremely zealous, yet their lives led to opposite outcomes. Zealous people have committed great atrocities, but they have also accomplished great good.

Similarly, zeal for God isn't automatically a positive trait. Counterfeit, unrighteous "zeal for God" has led people to stir up chaos and divisiveness and even to kill in his name. But true Christ-like zeal for God can lead one person to share food, clothing, and compassion with the "least of these," or give another person the courage to stand up and, reluctantly and with great gentleness, call out the church's sin.

Finally, zeal is redemptive. This is how Simon the Zealot becomes Simon the Zealot for the Kingdom. As I said, the positive value of zeal is in the eye of the beholder. And when Jesus beheld Simon, Scripture never indicates that he labeled Simon's zeal as sin, or instructed Simon to tone it down, or required Simon to change as a condition of acceptance. On the contrary, I think Jesus wanted Simon *for* his zeal. I think he wanted to use Simon's great passion to do great things. Simon is a reminder to us that Jesus does not want a soft, sanitized, well-mannered church, but a church that burns white-hot with the passion of God's love.

The redemptive potential of zeal, however, isn't always easy to see.

One Sunday afternoon a few years ago, my wife and I were visiting with family. We were having a very pleasant after-dinner conversation, and everything was going fine—until someone innocently touched one of my hot buttons.

I felt Monster Zeal come raging out of me. I struggled to recapture him and stuff him back in his cage, but when the discussion was over I felt icky.

As we drove home, my wife encouraged me, saying that she felt certain the debate had been a good one, and that I had not attacked anyone but had simply expressed my deeply held opinions in ways that were spirited, but not *mean*-spirited.

But I couldn't be sure; I didn't trust myself. Finally, I sighed in despair that I was certain my zeal would always lead me into embarrassment, or even sin, and I would never be able to conquer it.

Then my wife said quietly, "Dan, just give your zeal to Jesus."

I don't know exactly what that means, but I know it is right. I will never conquer my zeal. Instead, I must give it to Jesus.

I think that is ultimately the lesson of Simon's zeal: Jesus asked Simon not to give it up, but to give it to him.

4

THE SHADOW-DWELLER
A LIFETIME OF BEING UPSTAGED

I remember standing in a field on the hillside next to the church where I served as youth pastor for three years. I was with the senior pastor, who was approaching his third decade of service at the church, and he was telling me his dreams, his grand vision for this little church in the south hills of Missoula, Montana.

The church owned this field, now surrounded by hundreds of homes. The whole area had once been a cow pasture. Who could have dreamed that it would eventually become one of the fastest growing areas of town? The old German saint who donated the pasture did. So did my senior pastor.

As we stood on that hillside overlooking the Missoula Valley, he described his vision for the new sanctuary that would one day be built in this field, and how the current building would probably become the youth center. Since I was the youth pastor, that last part caught my attention and I began dreaming as well.

I remember asking him how many seats the new church would hold.

His answer surpassed my wildest imagination.

"A thousand," he said. At the time, I don't think there was any church that large in the entire area.

Time passed. I moved to Portland, Oregon, to attend seminary. Soon after, the senior pastor was elected to be the regional superintendent for our denomination, so he too moved away to accept his new role. Two couples—the pastor's son and daughter, who had both been in my youth group, and their spouses—stepped in to lead the church in Missoula.

And from Oregon, two states away, I watched and listened and monitored the progress as that little church on the hill swelled past the one-thousand-member mark, outgrowing the original building and field. I cheered as they sold that property, and bought and moved into a much bigger warehouse in town. The church was serving the community and getting noticed everywhere, even in the media.

I was thrilled to see that church make such an impact. It was, and still is, very exciting. Yet there was a frustration, an ache in the corner of my heart. As wonderful as it was to see and hear reports of this great dream coming true, I had longed to be there when it happened. I had envisioned myself helping to build the ministry, watering it and seeing it bloom and grow. I had worked expectantly, inside the church, watching for this vision to finally get traction and speed toward the horizon.

But God seemed to be calling me elsewhere.

As long as I thought I was fulfilling God's call for my life by working as a teacher and pursuing a PhD, I was happy to watch the Missoula church going gangbusters from several hundred miles away. But when both my teaching job and my PhD fell through and I was left with no dream of my own, I wrestled with the nagging idea that maybe I was such a loser that God needed to get me out of the way in order to grow the Missoula church. Such thoughts may sound silly, but they are a disturbing reality in the mind of a loser. The loser's logic is simple: knowing what I know about myself, why would God use *me* to do anything, when others are far more qualified, prepared, and willing? So I concluded that if I had stayed and tried to be part of the action, I probably would have interfered with the work and slowed things down.

I have always struggled with fears of being a shadow-dweller, watching from the stands as the real talent is out on the field, doing the important stuff. The exciting stuff. The stuff that matters.

Losers see themselves as being on the fringe, overshadowed by others who seem to have more gifts, more talent, more favor. Though the loser may possess some degree of skill, it always seems to be less than that of others. It's common for losers to feel that their best chance at making a meaningful contribution is to ride the coattails of others.

As I think about my life, I can honestly say that I have dwelt in the shadows of some pretty remarkable people. Some of them have great vision and talent, with big personalities and huge hearts to serve others. They are smart, passionate, and articulate. They possess tremendous knowledge and insight, as well as a keen grasp of the issues of the day. They are people I deeply love and respect—so much so, in fact, that I can feel intimidated by them.

What do they have that might make me feel that way?

Sometimes it's intellect. Besides trying to control Monster Zeal, another reason I sometimes stay in the shadows or remain quiet in discussions is because the level of discourse is out of my league and I simply can't think of anything to say.

Sometimes it's skills and achievements. Among my former classmates, there are lawyers, police officers, broadcast station managers, network journalists, social justice advocates, school principals, church planters, and at least one professional actor. By comparison, my work history has been mostly entry-level jobs and career changes. (The contrast makes for very awkward class reunions.)

Sometimes it's charisma. Some people have a glittering presence that cannot be ignored. They don't have to be loud and boisterous; they just naturally command attention. They are movers and shakers—shadow-casters, not shadow-dwellers—blazing their own trails, making their own news.

So, if others have more brains, talent, and magnetism than I, maybe I'm superfluous and the most helpful thing I can do is to step aside and let them get it done—right? After all, it's the American mantra: *Lead, follow, or get out of the way.*

I know, I know, this somewhat defeatist, "poor me" position denies all of the familiar biblical truths: God, not talent, determines our value; each gift, no matter how small, is just as important as the others; questioning our worth is an insult to God; envying the abilities of others is a sin. I have heard—I have *preached*—all of those truths. But to shadow-dwellers like me, those answers seem trite and unsatisfying, reaching the head but not the heart.

And the heart is where the shadow-dweller's struggle lies because the "loser's logic" does have a certain reason to it. After all, why *would* God pick an average Joe to fill a position that others are more qualified to fill? Why *would* he ask a shy introvert to lead, when scores of extroverts are more willing and able to do so? Why *would* he use the small, the timid, the ordinary, when everyone's attention is naturally drawn to the large, the brave, the spectacular?

I don't know; he just does.

Of all the people in the Bible, perhaps Andrew understood this better than anyone.

Andrew was a shadow-dweller—a second fiddle. True, Jesus did choose him to join the disciples, the circle of Jesus's twelve closest friends. But he was forever stuck in the shadow of one of those larger-than-life personalities: his famous brother, Simon Peter.

Every mention of Andrew in the Bible is phrased as either "Andrew, Simon Peter's brother," or worse, simply "Simon Peter's brother." So, throughout history, all who have ever known or heard of Andrew—the disciples, the gospel writers, and even we today— have always thought of him as subordinate to Peter. That is, if we think of him at all. (How many sermons or lessons have you seen or heard about Andrew? How many about Peter?)

I wonder what determined this pecking order. What was it that placed Andrew in Peter's shadow, and not vice versa? After all, who can imagine referring to Peter simply as "Andrew's brother"? Apparently the two brothers shared the same background and the same occupation as fishermen in the family fishing business. There is no mention in Scripture of any factors or advantages that would cause one brother to supersede the other. Neither seems to have any particular skills beyond fishing. Neither seems destined to rise above working-class status. Neither seems hierarchically superior to the other. And Scripture does not say which one was older.

So what made Peter the dominant sibling?

The only factor left, it seems, is personality.

I wonder how old Andrew was when he realized he would be forever in Peter's shadow. My guess is that he was young. In most families, it doesn't take long for people to start comparing the children: "If you study hard enough, maybe you can get into a good school like your sister," or "Joey has natural talent, but Susie is just different," or the dreaded, "Why can't you be more like ___?"

Was Andrew jealous? Did he try to escape Peter's shadow, or did he accept it early? Was he at peace with the realization that no matter what he did, Peter probably could do it with more flair?

And, going back to my earlier questions, why would Jesus need Andrew when someone like Peter was around? What could Andrew possibly add that Peter didn't already have covered?

For me, as I seek purpose while living in the shadows of others who shine more brightly, Andrew helps to illuminate those questions that have so troubled me. His life reveals much about the important work of the shadow-dweller. He has only three main "scenes" in Scripture—bringing Peter to Jesus, bringing the boy with the loaves and fishes to Jesus, and bringing some Greeks to Jesus—but in each case, he is introducing someone to Jesus.

Before we look at the first scene, it should be noted that the Gospels give different accounts of how Andrew and Peter started following Jesus. In Matthew 4:18 and Mark 1:16, Jesus calls them together, while they are fishing. But the gospel of John implies that they had met him before then:

> The next day John [the Baptist] was there again
> with two of his disciples. When he saw Jesus passing

by, he said, "Look, the Lamb of God!" When the two disciples heard him say this, they followed Jesus. Turning around, Jesus saw them following and asked, "What do you want?" They said, "Rabbi" (which means "Teacher"), "where are you staying?" "Come," he replied, "and you will see." So they went and saw where he was staying, and they spent that day with him. It was about four in the afternoon. Andrew, Simon Peter's brother, was one of the two who heard what John had said and who had followed Jesus. The first thing Andrew did was to find his brother Simon and tell him, "We have found the Messiah" (that is, the Christ). And he brought him to Jesus. (1:35–42)

Note the two brothers' different styles. Andrew is a natural evangelist, but without fanfare. He announces the fulfillment of all the hopes and longings of the nation of Israel, down through the centuries, in just five words: "We have found the Messiah." Compare this delivery to Peter's long, expressive speeches (such as in Acts 1:15–22; 2:14–41; 3:12–26; and 4:8–12) and try to imagine Peter simply stating, "We have found the Messiah."

Go ahead, try it.

And yet in this passage, it's because of Andrew, the second fiddle, that Peter meets Jesus.

That blows my mind. Think of Peter—all his stories, all his drama, all his antics. Then consider this: if not for Andrew's introduction, Peter might never have met Jesus.

The next time Andrew appears, he is again acting as a facilitator:

When Jesus looked up and saw a great crowd coming toward him, he said to Philip, "Where shall we buy bread for these people to eat?" He asked this only to test him, for he already had in mind what he was going to do. Philip answered him, "It would take more than half a year's wages to buy enough bread for each one to have a bite!" Another of his disciples, Andrew, Simon Peter's brother, spoke up, "Here is a boy with five small barley loaves and two small fish, but how far will they go among so many?" Jesus said, "Have the people sit down." There was plenty of grass in that place, and they sat down (about five thousand men were there). Jesus then took the loaves, gave thanks, and distributed to those who were seated as much as they wanted. He did the same with the fish. When they had all had enough to eat, he said to his disciples, "Gather the pieces that are left over. Let nothing be wasted." So they gathered them and filled twelve baskets with the pieces of the five barley loaves left over by those who had eaten. (John 6:5–13)

Again, note the contrast between Andrew and Philip. In response to Jesus's question, Philip—the accountant, the bean counter, the numbers cruncher—makes a quick mental calculation and dramatically explains the enormity of the problem: "It would take more than half a year's wages to buy enough bread for each one to have a bite!" In the New International Version of the Bible, the translators capture Philip's intensity with an exclamation point. The more tentative

Andrew, however, merits not an exclamation point but a question mark: "Here is a boy with five small barley loaves and two small fish, but how far will they go among so many?"

So, among the disciples, it appears that Andrew has even less charisma than the bean counter.

Now *that's* saying something.

But I wonder—would that little boy have offered his lunch to any other disciple? As I look at the disciples' reactions to children at other times (Matt. 19:13–14; Mark 10:13–14; Luke 18:15–16), I imagine they might have said something like, "Beat it, kid! Jesus is far too important to bother with silly suggestions from a squirt like you." Maybe Andrew thought so too but lacked the nerve to say so. Maybe the only reason Andrew brought the boy to Jesus was because he couldn't think of anything else to do.

What matters is, he did it. And the rest of the Scripture passage reveals the miracle that followed: the feeding of the five thousand.

Andrew's third scene is when a group of Greeks ask to see Jesus, and Philip and Andrew deliver the message:

> Now there were some Greeks among those who went up to worship at the festival. They came to Philip, who was from Bethsaida in Galilee, with a request. "Sir," they said, "we would like to see Jesus." Philip went to tell Andrew; Andrew and Philip in turn told Jesus. Jesus replied, "The hour has come for the Son of Man to be glorified. Very truly I tell you, unless a kernel of wheat falls to the ground and dies, it remains only a single seed. But if it dies, it produces many seeds. Anyone who

loves their life will lose it, while anyone who hates their life in this world will keep it for eternal life. Whoever serves me must follow me; and where I am, my servant also will be. My Father will honor the one who serves me. Now my soul is troubled, and what shall I say? 'Father, save me from this hour'? No, it was for this very reason I came to this hour. Father, glorify your name!" Then a voice came from heaven, "I have glorified it, and will glorify it again." The crowd that was there and heard it said it had thundered; others said an angel had spoken to him. Jesus said, "This voice was for your benefit, not mine. Now is the time for judgment on this world; now the prince of this world will be driven out. And I, when I am lifted up from the earth, will draw all people to myself." He said this to show the kind of death he was going to die. (John 12:20–33)

Notice how this passage reports *that* Andrew and Philip told Jesus about the Greeks, but not *what* they actually said. If the Greeks had made initial contact with Peter, I'm sure Peter would have been quoted—because in Scripture, Peter is always saying something quotable. He never seems to stay on the sidelines; he's just too big to go unnoticed.

Andrew, on the other hand, seems to have developed the skill of dwelling gracefully in the shadows, deferring to someone greater. As a child, he learned to dwell in Peter's shadow. As an adult, he dwelt in John the Baptist's. And when Jesus finally appeared, Andrew shifted quietly to dwelling in the shadow of the Savior (John 1:35–40).

Just look at the ripples of impact from Andrew's introductions of other people to Jesus.

- Peter is presented in Acts as one of the great leaders of the church, standing up to the Jewish leaders who crucified Jesus and preaching to thousands throughout Jerusalem and Palestine (Acts 2:14–41; 4:8–17).
- The little boy becomes known throughout history as the one whose lunch miraculously fed five thousand people. We don't know what became of him, but surely he was changed by this amazing event and went on to tell others.
- The Greeks must have talked about Jesus to everyone they knew, especially if they were present to hear the voice that came from heaven immediately after they asked to see him (John 12:22–33).

All of these effects took place because Andrew, the shadow-dweller, stepped back and introduced others to Jesus.

Andrew does not have Peter's power to evangelize huge crowds, but he has the power to motivate Peter to get up and go meet Jesus in the first place. He has the power to make a little boy feel safe enough to offer his tiny lunch to Jesus. He has the power to welcome a group of Greeks—Gentiles—who might have been rejected by Peter (Peter had trouble with Gentiles, as seen in Acts 10 and Galatians 2).

True, society may celebrate people with big personalities, and the bigger the better; but to many of us, they seem out of reach. Something about their bigness makes us feel smaller.

I once took my nephew to a training camp of our favorite NFL team. We watched the team work out, do drills, and scrimmage. These were professionals, the best of the best. They had even been to the Super Bowl the previous season.

I was in awe.

After practice each day, they headed to the showers by way of a sidewalk roped off from us. Some players walked along the ropes and signed autographs. I got many autographs from first-string players, but I also noticed something: in their presence I turned into an overexcited six-year-old, jumping up and down, pleading with men ten years my junior to sign a little football.

Then the head coach walked by.

A hush fell over the crowd. We were in the presence of greatness.

After the team disappeared inside, I regained my ability to form complete sentences. I realized then that all of those men were larger than life, able to reduce their adult fans to giddy children.

In Scripture Andrew, the shadow-dweller, does not have that effect on people. He is safe, trustworthy, approachable. People who want to see Jesus are attracted to Andrew.

Wouldn't it be great if the same could be said about each one of us?

Think about other shadow-dwellers who sparked great miracles and movements in the church. For instance, who introduced Billy Graham, the best-known evangelist of the twentieth century, to Jesus? (It was a traveling evangelist named Mordecai Ham—a shadow-dweller next to Graham, but look at the impact of that introduction.) Who mentored C. S. Lewis, certainly one of the greatest and most prolific Christian writers of the twentieth century? (It was Charles Williams—a successful author in his own right, but much less famous than Lewis.) Who discipled towering theological leaders and reformers like Martin Luther, John Wesley, Dwight Moody, Jonathan Edwards, Martin Luther King Jr., and scores of others in their spiritual journeys? With a bit of research, we could find out—but their names certainly aren't household names. Like Andrew, each of them was a shadow-dweller who paved the way for someone greater.

Andrew reveals a pattern throughout Scripture and church history: somewhere behind every great spiritual leader, there is usually a spiritually sensitive shadow-dweller.

Composer Leonard Bernstein put it this way: "I can get plenty of first violinists, but to find someone who plays second violin with as much enthusiasm ... now that's a problem. And yet if no one plays second, we have no harmony."[1]

The superstar is enhanced by the sidekick, the facilitator, the second banana.

This forces me, as a shadow-dweller, to rethink my place in the church in Montana. Maybe I did play a part in that church becoming what it is today. Maybe some spark from my little youth group lay dormant and flared up only after I left.

Maybe some prayers I prayed were answered.

Maybe I am a part of it, after all.

5

THE BIGOT

ADMIT IT, YOU'RE ONE TOO

On July 7, 2005, I was on the Eurostar train from Paris to London, speeding beneath the English Channel. The train had been delayed for about an hour near Calais, the last stop in France, due to something that was happening in London—but we were not told what it was.

After emerging from the Chunnel in Ashford, a town on the southern coast of England, the train came to a halt—again, with no explanation—and a voice over the PA system offered us the option of taking another train back to France, free of charge.

At about that time, people's cell phones started ringing with calls from family and friends. Dialogue dulled to ominous whispers.

From the incoming calls, we learned that there had been an explosion—no, several explosions—in London. At first, it sounded like a problem in the power grid. But when we heard of travel alerts warning people not to enter London, the situation began to sound more grave.

Something sinister was happening.

Before boarding the Eurostar, I had left my wife and my French-speaking sister-in-law at Charles de Gaulle Airport in Paris. Since I had no French speakers with me, I decided that instead of returning to France, I'd stick with my original schedule and stay in England. Further, since London is the central transportation hub in southern England and I didn't know where else to go, I decided to continue toward London, one cautious step at a time.

As the train pulled into Waterloo Station, the streets of London were frighteningly bare. As soon as I got off the train, I started to see breaking headlines on newsstands and TV screens about what was happening. According to the news, three explosive devices had detonated on three different subways, and a fourth had blown the top off of a double-decker bus.

All of these explosions were just minutes apart. All had been confirmed to be the work of Muslim suicide bombers.

More terrifying details followed. When I asked about getting to Euston Station, I learned that the bomb on the double-decker bus had detonated only blocks from there, so that station was closed. However, I was able to secure an alternate train route that ran west from Waterloo Station to Oxford and then headed north—the direction I wanted to go. I got my ticket, boarded the train, and made it safely to Birmingham.

I was filled with relief and thanksgiving.

A couple of days later, as Londoners tried to catch their breath, I went in to the Birmingham City Centre to get some supplies and take in a movie. I didn't encounter any problems, but the next day my email was flooded with urgent messages from family members, asking if I was all right. Apparently, shortly after I returned from the movie theater, thousands of people were evacuated from the City Centre when a suspicious device was found aboard a double-decker bus, though it later turned out to be nothing. Unbeknownst to me, news stations across the United States had been broadcasting the entire evacuation in real time; I missed all the activity by about one hour.

Birmingham has one of the highest Muslim populations in the United Kingdom, and some of the suspects implicated in those July 7 bombings—British citizens of Middle Eastern descent—were later apprehended and arrested in Birmingham.

Two weeks passed without incident, and things seemed to settle down. People were resuming their everyday routines. I was preparing to return to London for some sightseeing. I had tickets for a couple of theater productions and a riverboat cruise through the city, and I was excited.

London has a special place in my heart!

But the day before I left, my wife emailed me, thinking I was already in London. Again, she was asking if I was all right. Three more detonators had exploded around the city. Mercifully, the explosives themselves had failed to go off and no one was hurt, but everyone was rattled.

The attacks were not over.

Everyone wondered whether to expect more.

However, after consideration, I decided not to cancel my trip to London. Like many others, I felt that ceasing to "live my life" was letting terrorism win. So off I went.

On the day of my cruise down the Thames, I boarded the riverboat, choosing a seat on the upper deck toward the back of the boat where I could snap photos of famous landmarks.

At a stop near the Tower of London, three young people—two women and a man—boarded the boat and took seats right across from me. Judging from their language and appearance, they seemed to be Middle Eastern. And they all carried backpacks.

Suddenly, I didn't feel as safe as before.

I tried to continue my tour as normally as possible. But—I hate to admit this—the whole time they were on the boat, I felt uneasy. I kept glancing sideways at them, instinctively tensing up whenever they moved. I knew my thoughts were crazy and unfair, but I couldn't quiet them.

I even formulated a "just in case" escape plan. I decided that if I saw anything even remotely suspicious, I would leap over the railing into the river.

Thank goodness I was able to quickly distinguish benign objects from explosive devices. At a couple of points, when the foreigners did reach into their pockets or backpacks, I would have looked pretty foolish diving into the water to escape from a cell phone—or a sandwich.

Did my fearful profiling make me a racist? Some might say no. After all, it was a scary time. Everyone knew London and Birmingham had suffered multiple attacks. No one knew if more attacks were planned. I was just staying aware of my surroundings. How could such due diligence be considered bigotry?

Maybe that argument is valid—but I'm not so sure.

I stereotyped three total strangers as undesirable, maybe even dangerous, and was ready to believe the worst possible things about them—with no evidence at all. I was even ready to jump overboard if they tried anything funny. And all because of how they looked, how they talked.

I don't know, maybe my response was diligence, but I think it was bigotry.

This chapter is harder to write than some earlier chapters, which were about types of people to whom we all can relate. Being a nobody, a shadow-dweller, or even a zealot isn't so bad; those traits are just quirks. Even being biased or narrow-minded isn't completely beyond the pale, because such traits could in some cases reflect a well-considered position that can be defended.

But being a bigot? It's a reputation that, once it sticks to you, cannot be shaken off.

Want to ruin someone's reputation, someone's career? Just call him or her a bigot. It doesn't even have to be true; all you have to do is *say* it's true. It's the kiss of death.

Bigots are our modern-day pariahs, shunned by society. If you can successfully label a person a bigot—justifiably or not—you can discredit anything he or she will ever say or do, no matter how valid it might be.

A bigot is avoided.

Ostracized.

Exiled.

And as I look in the mirror—pierced by my own bigotry—I would love to steer clear of this, to soften it somehow, to point it out in others without examining it in myself.

When we think of bigotry, it is easy to think of extremes down through history: Nazism in Europe, lynch mobs in the United States, genocide in Africa. With all my heart, I believe that these chapters in history are shameful and unrighteous. So when the light of Scripture reveals bigotry in *me*, I feel very uncomfortable.

Merriam-Webster defines a bigot as "a person who is obstinately or intolerantly devoted to his or her own opinions and prejudices; *especially*: one who regards or treats the members of a group (as a racial or ethnic group) with hatred and intolerance."[1]

But the definition goes beyond racial discrimination. Note that the main definition is one who is "obstinately or intolerantly devoted to his or her own opinions and prejudices."

No one escapes that definition. We are all bigots—just in different areas.

Take the area of politics. Some Democrats believe that all Republicans are wrong on all issues, and some Republicans believe the same about all Democrats. Each sees the other as unpatriotic, unintelligent, unenlightened. Each thinks the other is the problem.

But, you may be thinking, surely I'm not saying that having a political opinion can morph into bigotry?

Yes, I am. Read the primary definition again. It's fine to believe in a particular political position or ideology; but if you secretly view those who disagree as less evolved, less rational—if you joke with your pals about "those people"—then yes, you are indeed a bigot.

In my life, the issue of homelessness has provided two interesting case studies about bigotry—one on the East Coast and one on the West—on two different sides of the issue. First, the East Coast story.

I had taken my youth group to Washington, D.C., for a Christian conference, and we were eating lunch at a snack bar near the Washington Monument. As we ate, we were approached by a stranger with a wad of cash in his hand. He said he was collecting donations for a program to help homeless people get off the street.

Caught off guard, we didn't say anything right away.

At that, assuming we weren't going to give him anything, he smirked, "I died and went to Republican heaven."

Now, since we're talking about bigotry, I don't want to show bigotry against *him*, so I won't belabor the fact that our tour guides had warned us against letting clever panhandlers guilt us into coughing up cash. But if he really believed what he said—that all people who fail to give money to strangers on the street *must* be heartless, and *must* be Republicans—then he was a bigot. He had never met us, and he didn't know our giving habits or voting records. Yet he made a sweeping generalization about us before we spoke a single word.

Shady as he may have been, though, maybe he had a point: I haven't always been free of bigotry, even against the homeless. And that brings me to the other case study, this time on the West Coast.

I grew up hearing and believing that all homeless people are just lazy—they've made poor choices, they drain local resources, they are an embarrassment. To me, the solution was simple: just get a job.

Then, in seminary, I led a service trip to inner city Los Angeles. One morning, I ate breakfast at a soup kitchen with a man named Earl, who had lived on the street for years. Inside I had some of the judgmental thoughts I just mentioned, but fortunately the Holy Spirit protected Earl by keeping my mouth clamped shut.

As Earl shared his story, he mentioned that he had two daughters in Dallas, Texas, whom he hadn't seen in ten years.

"Why haven't you tried to contact them?" I asked.

Looking down at his plate, he said, "Because I don't feel worthy to be called their father."

A couple of days later, our group stopped for dinner and our local guide ordered a second meal to go. As I drove the van back to our quarters, she asked me to pull over at a certain street corner, where a man sat hidden in the shadows. Silently, she climbed out, placed the food before him, and returned to the van.

He barely acknowledged her presence.

As we drove away, our guide told us that people in the area called this man Sunshine or Brother, but he had never told any of them his real name.

A girl from the back of the van asked why.

Our guide, staring straight ahead, replied, "Because he doesn't believe he's worthy to have a name."

In my bigotry, I had believed laziness to be the only causative factor in the problem of homelessness. But Earl and Brother taught me that the true cause is much deeper. It is brokenness: broken people, broken society. And the solution is Jesus—the very Jesus in me.

My understanding of homelessness was expanded during that trip. Unfortunately, that does not mean that bigotry is never a problem anymore. It still bubbles within me, within all of us, and it is hard to face.

Bigotry isn't limited to politics or social issues. It can appear in almost any area: sports, education, religion. As explained earlier, my bigotry sometimes comes out in the form of Monster Zeal. When I meet Christians who see things differently than I do, I've tried to break the habit of making that awful bigoted statement: "How can anyone believe *that* and still claim to be a Christian?" But at times, unfortunately, I still think it. And after years of observing people, I can state unequivocally that bigotry is present among progressives and conservatives alike.

I was forced to confront my bigotry when I met Jesus in the form of three tourists in London and two homeless men in L.A. The disciple Nathanael[2] was forced to confront his bigotry when he met Jesus in person.

In John 1 Nathanael's friend Philip makes the claim of a lifetime: he has found the Messiah!

But Nathanael's response and Jesus's reply are a bit unexpected.

Philip found Nathanael and told him, "We have found the one Moses wrote about in the Law, and about whom the prophets also wrote—Jesus of Nazareth, the son of Joseph."

"Nazareth! Can anything good come from there?" Nathanael asked.

"Come and see," said Philip.

When Jesus saw Nathanael approaching, he said of him, "Here truly is an Israelite in whom there is no deceit."

"How do you know me?" Nathanael asked.

Jesus answered, "I saw you while you were still under the fig tree before Philip called you."

Then Nathanael declared, "Rabbi, you are the Son of God; you are the king of Israel."

Jesus said, "You believe because I told you I saw you under the fig tree. You will see greater things than that." He then added, "Very truly I tell you, you will see 'heaven open, and the angels of God ascending and descending on' the Son of Man." (vv. 45–51)

Nathanael is so anti-Nazareth that he almost misses the greatest opportunity of his life. Scripture doesn't explain the basis of his sentiment, but probably it was because Nazareth at that time was an obscure, insignificant town, populated mostly by manual laborers who didn't have money, status, or power. You could say Nathanael considered them hicks.

I believe Nathanael's bigotry was regional, cultural, economic, and intellectual. His put-down of Nazareth shows sarcasm, which requires wit and intelligence, so I think he probably had some education and felt intellectually superior to those rubes from Nazareth.

Let's look for a moment at the kind of bigotry that is based on intellect or academics. I've been on both sides of that kind.

First, I truly believe that academic bigotry was at least one of the factors in play during my oral defense. If so, then I can attest that it is very painful to be on the receiving end.

Second, in my years as a graduate student, post-graduate student, and college teacher, I have been around education and academia long enough to see many variations of intellectual bigotry. The more awards received, degrees earned, and books published, the greater the temptation to feel superior—even spiritually superior—to others, despite the fact that such attitudes are totally incompatible with Christlikeness.

Third, after losing my PhD in such a dramatic and humiliating way, I wish I could say that I have been forever broken of those attitudes; but incredibly, I can't. Believe it or not, sometimes I still catch myself feeling superior, for one petty reason or another. And each time, I feel ashamed—ashamed of quashing the Jesus in me that others might see.

Yet look how graciously Jesus works with bigots. In this story, Jesus praises Nathanael's honesty and reveals that he truly *sees* Nathanael for what he is.

And in this moment of grace, Nathanael is stunned into total belief and submission. He forgets his societal prejudices and becomes a citizen of a new society: the kingdom of heaven.

Once freed of his bigotry, Nathanael apparently spent the rest of his life following Jesus and introducing others to him.

Jesus can redeem and use anyone—even a bigot.

Like Nathanael.

Like me.

6

THE PRAGMATIST
TOO PRACTICAL TO DREAM BIG

You might find it strange that this chapter is titled The Pragmatist, thinking it sounds a bit out of place in a book about losers.

A pragmatist might be considered a thinker, a planner, a self-starter who uses common sense to successfully navigate life's ups and downs. And living pragmatically—making decisions based on logic and principle—might be considered a desirable path, likely to lead to a peaceful, stable life.

By contrast, the non-pragmatist might be considered flighty and unrealistic, living in a world of fancy and fantasy—a dreamer, a sucker, a flake—someone to keep on a tight leash, lest he or she squander valuable resources, like time and money.

So can a pragmatist be a loser?

Well, yes. Like all personality traits, pragmatism is both a strength and a weakness. It can lead to stability and good decisions, but it can also stifle the ability to be creative and take risks when needed. In the case of the pragmatic disciple Philip, it almost caused him to miss the miracles that were happening all around him.

A pragmatist deals in reality—what *is,* not what might be. In a crisis, she will assess the situation, execute the most logical solution, and then move on and never look back. For example, in the case of unemployment, she might take a day or two to analyze lessons learned from the previous job, assess personal strengths and weaknesses (probably side by side, in a two-column table), and formulate new goals and objectives for the next phase of life. She is proactive: collecting letters of reference, updating her résumé, seeking help from employment agencies and career counseling services. That's developing a plan. That's how a pragmatist might look for a new job.

But that's not how I do it.

I am more of a backdoor, upside-down pragmatic. By backdoor, I mean that I wasn't born one, like Philip; instead, I became one through hardship. By upside-down, I mean that I do live by a set of principles, like a true pragmatist; but unfortunately those principles are more nihilistic than formulaic. My main life principle is that stuff just happens. You can work hard, get an education, and do whatever it takes to better yourself, and life can still cut you off at the ankles. Sometimes, no matter what you do, it might not be enough. Everything is out of your control. Being good and doing the right thing is no guarantee. You may be at the top, but nothing lasts forever.

This kind of pragmatism, bordering on nihilism, can sound pretty depressing—especially coming from a Christ-follower. But since we are talking about pragmatism, I have to be pragmatic and admit this reality because I have experienced it firsthand.

I didn't just wake up one day and decide that life stinks. Instead,

I developed my nihilistic pragmatism as a way to cope with grief and pain because it offered a numbing stability when I felt my life spinning out of control.

I don't defend this philosophy. I don't justify it.

It just is.

Each of us has a worldview—a fishbowl—made up of our past and present. We each live in our own fishbowl and view the world through it. Our families, our faiths, our cultures, our experiences have helped to construct this fishbowl through which we perceive reality. Months, and even years, after I lost my job, my PhD, and my future, I began to realize—mostly through conversations with others—the kind of fishbowl through which I look at the world.

My fishbowl is constructed to filter out all that is positive; only the negative gets through. This is why the judgments of just three people—my two doctoral examiners and one former boss—were able to sink in so deeply and outweigh all of the encouragement from scores of other friends and relatives, students, and bosses—past and present. My fishbowl, constructed by my trauma, filters out that encouragement.

As I look at Philip, I am learning how much trauma has affected, and still affects, my worldview. How can I, a seminary graduate, Christian teacher, and Bible instructor, be such a nihilist? Conversely, how can a nihilist like me ever proclaim the good news of the gospel? How can I share the love of God with others when sometimes I can barely see it myself? Surely I won't be eligible for ministry until this serious flaw is overcome.

But is overcoming my nihilism even possible? I mean, I could pretend. Pretend that everything's fine, that no struggle exists, that life is hunky-dory. There are enough pretenders in the body of Christ.

Simply leaping out of my current worldview and into another seems just as impossible as a fish leaping from its fishbowl to discover the reality of dryness. How does a nihilistic pragmatic, or any pragmatic, allow illogical miracles, impractical grace, and irrational love to penetrate a fishbowl that took a whole lifetime to construct?

Yet Jesus called a pragmatic to be his disciple. Again, at first this seems like a strength—not a loser characteristic. Philip is detail-oriented, meticulous, precise. He tells Nathanael, "We have found the one Moses wrote about in the Law, and about whom the prophets also wrote—Jesus of Nazareth, the son of Joseph" (John 1:45). Unlike Andrew's simple statement to Peter—"We have found the Messiah" (John 1:41)—Philip details the ancient prophecies and Jesus's origins. He mentions Moses, the Law, the prophets, and even who Jesus's father is. Note that in order to relate that last detail, he had to do some fact-checking. Textbook-like, he includes the most detailed and accurate information possible in order to rule out any ambiguity, misinterpretation, or loopholes.

Philip brings an analytical mind to the group. He is the bean counter, the numbers cruncher. Though his spirit affirms that Jesus is the Messiah, his mind finds Jesus's methods abstract and hard to understand. So Philip responds with practical questions that everyone else is either too reluctant or too clueless to bring up. His spirit tells him exactly who Jesus is, but his mind—like mine, filled with hard-nosed realism—doesn't quite get it.

In fact, every time we see Philip in the Gospels, he is on the verge of missing a blessing because of his pragmatism. His practicality, a real asset in an accounting firm or an engineering group, becomes a liability when a miracle is in the works.

This point first comes into view when Jesus feeds five thousand people—a story, told in all four Gospels (Matt. 14:13–21; Mark 6:32–44; Luke 9:10–17; John 6:1–13), in which the crowds follow Jesus past the Sea of Galilee to a remote mountainside where there is no food.

In an apparent side note, the Gospels tell us that at this particular time, Jesus has been performing many signs and healings (Matt. 14:14; John 6:2). Hold that thought—it's not a side note at all. It will be very important in just a moment.

The Sea of Galilee is actually a lake, with a perimeter of about thirty miles, and Scripture indicates that Jesus didn't stop until he had traveled some distance beyond it. So people had to walk, or run (Mark 6:33), about fifteen miles to get around the lake and then climb an unknown distance up into the hills.

Quite a trek.

Very calorie-burning.

Very hunger-inducing.

As the masses approach, Jesus fires off a practical question to the pragmatic Philip: "Where shall we buy bread for these people to eat?" (John 6:5). And for all the pragmatic readers who would read this account down through the ages, the next verse explains that Jesus "asked this only to test him, for he already had in mind what he was going to do."

Here's what Jesus wanted to know: Would Philip see the problem through spiritual eyes, understanding how big God truly is—or through natural eyes, viewing it as an impossible task?

You know the answer. True to form, the practical Philip fails Jesus's test. Instead of believing that God can do miracles, his analytical mind swings into action, reframing the question as a fifth-grade story problem: if a loaf of bread costs *x* dollars, and each loaf can feed *y* people, how many loaves and how much money would it take to feed five thousand?

Overwhelmed by his own calculations, Philip blurts in exasperation: "It would take more than half a year's wages to buy enough bread for each one to have a bite!" (v. 7).

But Jesus's point is that the situation does not call for practical calculations.

Remember how the Scripture said Jesus had been performing a lot of signs and healings? Most of these miracles were performed in public. Everyone saw them. That's why the crowds were flocking to Jesus. And Scripture indicates that the disciples were with Jesus during this period, so Philip must have seen them too.

The signs.

The healings.

The miracles.

And yet, in an instant, he forgets them all.

Philip is so pragmatic that he sees only the obstacle of what *is*. He cannot imagine what *could be*, even when the solution—Jesus, the miracle worker—is standing right in front of him.

Philip sees only the actual, not the possible.

As I discussed in the story of Andrew, we know what happened: Jesus prayed over one little boy's lunch, and it multiplied to feed the entire crowd.

Amazing!

But if I had been standing in Philip's sandals, gazing at a sea of five thousand famished faces out on a lonely mountain, wouldn't I too have tried to solve the problem by human calculations? Doesn't my nihilistic pragmatism keep me always focused on the next obstacle rather than on Jesus, the solution? And don't I always hear that practical voice in my head, telling me I dare not hope for a miracle?

How many times, after Jesus has tested me and proven himself to me, have I been clueless again the next time he turns around?

Fortunately, Jesus showed grace and patience to Philip during this test. As many times as my pragmatism has caused me to fail similar tests, I can only be assured that this same grace and patience will cover me too.

The next time Philip appears in the Gospels, once again he almost misses a blessing because of his pragmatism. It's the incident in which some Greeks approach Philip, asking to see Jesus (John 12:20–22).

And what does Philip do?

He passes them off to Andrew.

Why doesn't Philip take them to Jesus himself?

I am sure it was not because the disciples had a protocol for screening seekers before bringing them to Jesus; any such protocol would violate Jesus's lifelong pattern of welcoming everyone freely, without obstacles. And we know it wasn't because Philip was too busy to handle the request, because, after delivering the Greeks to Andrew to take to Jesus, Philip goes with them anyway.

So why does Philip hesitate and consult Andrew?

Perhaps Philip is confused by a culture clash that just doesn't make sense to him. Perhaps he can't imagine why these foreigners would want to speak with the Jewish Messiah, or perhaps he fears that Jesus might not want to see them. Personally, I think Philip can't see any legitimate reason for the Greeks to meet Jesus, and yet he doesn't want to be the one to make that call. So he hands them over to Andrew. Then he goes with them anyway. That way, if the meeting turns out well he can share the credit; and if not, he won't be blamed for making an error in judgment.

I give Philip credit: Despite his indecisiveness, he did perform an assist in bringing the Greeks to Jesus. He did *something*, which is more than I often do. However, he seems almost paralyzed by self-doubt and second-guessing. Pragmatists can overanalyze a situation until they are frozen in fear. Walking with Jesus requires a journey into the unknown, and that can be very scary for a pragmatist.

For months after the loss of my PhD and my dream job, I received rejection after rejection of my job applications. No one wanted to interview me. No one wanted *me*.

After a year, an email came to inquire if I would be interested in teaching a class at a local university. Like Philip passing the Greeks to Andrew, I passed the email to my wife. I had been rejected in the most humiliating ways, at every level of education—both as a high-school teacher and as a PhD candidate. My self-confidence had hit rock bottom. I kept thinking, *What could I possibly bring to this university? Do they know how much of a loser I am?* I was sure that if they knew my whole story, they would never consider hiring me.

I almost ignored the invitation. I was frozen. Fortunately, like Andrew, my wife took the handoff and ran with it, heaping loads of encouragement upon me. She had no doubt I could teach at the college level. I had every doubt in the world. Most of her encouragement bounced off of me, but just enough seeped in for me to follow through.

That semester I was hired to teach one class. In the semesters that followed, I was asked to teach a second class, then a third, then a fourth, and since then I have happily continued to teach various classes on an adjunct (as-needed) basis. All the while, I have continued to doubt myself, still wondering how I can teach at the college level without a PhD. But God continues to make a way, despite all my doubts and fears—and despite the obvious gap in my credentials.

How many Christians today would love to hear a group of as-yet-unbelievers say, in so many words, "Can you please introduce us to Jesus?" Leading people to Jesus—isn't that what we Christ-followers are all about? But Philip didn't grab this chance of a lifetime. Instead, like me, he wavered, probably because he feared being rejected or making a mistake. He doubted his own judgment. He froze.

Pragmatism can do that to you. It can blind you to the great work God is doing.

This leads us to the final example of Philip's pragmatism. Jesus and his disciples are in Jerusalem for Passover. The Jewish religious leaders are pitted against Jesus, and the situation seems to be getting serious. The disciples' comments at the Last Supper make it clear that they are hoping Jesus will reveal himself to the world in a way that everyone can understand, like emerging as a great king or political leader. Then Philip steps up and makes a seemingly reasonable request: "Lord, show us the Father and that will be enough for us" (John 14:8).

Surely there's nothing wrong with that. Surely the desire to draw closer to God is a worthy one.

The problem is, Philip's request reveals his inability to connect the dots. Jesus has just said, "I am the way and the truth and the life. No one comes to the Father except through me. If you really know me, you will know my Father as well. From now on, you do know him and have seen him" (vv. 6–7).

In Western culture, we usually think of knowing as something cognitive—an exercise in fact gathering. We make observations and create hypotheses ("The floor looks wet; maybe something is leaking") and verify them with our five senses ("Yes, I feel it; this water pipe is dripping").

But knowing is more than facts. To say I know my wife simply because I see her every day isn't very meaningful. Nor is it very romantic. No, I know my wife because I have loved her, lived with her, talked with her, and walked the road of life with her for many years. This is what Jesus means by knowing the Father.

This interaction between Jesus and Philip takes place at the very end of Jesus's ministry, on the night before he is crucified. For three years, Philip has known him intimately, seen and heard his teachings in action, and watched him perform miraculous signs of the kingdom of God.

Yet Philip wants just one more sign. One more miracle. One more confirmation. The three years, the countless miracles, the life with Jesus, isn't enough. Philip needs just one more act, and he thinks that will finally be enough.

Enough to accept.

Enough to believe.

But how much is enough? How many signs and miracles does it take to finally start seeing God?

At first glance, I am embarrassed for Philip, exposed in his unbelief. I think to myself, *If I had walked with Jesus, I would believe after the very first miracle—the first storm pacified, the first demoniac healed, the first dead person raised. I would never ask Jesus for just one more sign in order to believe.*

But after a second look, I am embarrassed for *myself.* For thinking I would be different than Philip. I typically place a lot of emphasis on the physical reality around me. I am human, after all.

It's easy to say that faith is believing what we cannot see. It's much harder to actually live it.

In the movie *Indiana Jones and the Last Crusade*, Indiana must cross a great chasm to save his father's life. He cannot go forward, but he cannot turn back. Reading from a mysterious book, he finds one cryptic clue: "Only in the leap from the lion's head will he prove his worth."

In an instant, looking out over the uncrossable chasm, he understands: it's a leap of faith.

He clutches his chest, sets his jaw, and steps off the lion's head into nothing. But instead of free-falling into the abyss, his weight lands on a bridge that appears only when his foot touches it.

When facing a chasm, how many of us have asked for one more sign, one more indication that God is with us? I know I have. I have been a Christian for most of my life—years and years—and frankly God has done some wonderful things. At each major crossroads, he has maneuvered my life in ways that, though painful, have led to greater things. Time after time. Yet no matter how many times I have seen God perform wonders through the dark times in my past, and even my present, I always seek one more sign.

Just one more to finally see and believe.

I hate to admit that my faith journey is more like an endless loop than a forward progression. My faith gets tested; I fail miserably. I learn from the event, thinking, *Now I get it!* I come to the next chasm, which requires the next step of faith. And I fail miserably again.

I'm in the middle of my life, and I have yet to break this cycle.

If I were Indiana Jones, standing at the edge of the chasm, I would not take that leap; I'd cut and run. Sure, I can trust Christ to save me and forgive my sin. I can acknowledge his leading, guidance, and protection in the past. But the moment I stand before an impossible abyss, all those memories blow away, like dust clouds over the prairie. I no longer see the many signs he has given me; I see only the precipice before me.

And I am scared.

So I ask for one more sign.

I understand Philip's quandary. I cannot fault him for requesting one more sign, even though the very Son of God is right beside him.

Jesus responds to Philip directly: "Don't you know me, Philip, even after I have been among you such a long time? Anyone who has seen me has seen the Father. How can you say, 'Show us the Father'?" (John 14:9).

Jesus acknowledges Philip's pragmatism—his need for physical evidence—and offers reminders of such evidence: "Believe me when I say that I am in the Father and the Father is in me; or at least believe on the evidence of the miracles themselves" (v. 11). Philip saw those miracles, and Jesus says that is enough physical evidence. But then Jesus challenges Philip to "see" beyond the physical:

> Very truly I tell you, whoever believes in me will do the works I have been doing, and they will do even greater things than these, because I am going to the Father. And I will do whatever you ask in my name, so that the Father may be glorified in the Son. You may ask me for anything in my name, and I will do it. (vv. 12–14)

Fortunately, Jesus approaches the pragmatist with patience—and a challenge to go beyond.

When I began this chapter, I thought I would have a hard time identifying with Philip, the pragmatist. Yet below the surface, I share Philip's struggle. When all is said and done, I focus far more on physical obstacles than on spiritual truths. I spend more time on calculating the impossibilities than on releasing them to an infinite God.

Like Philip, when spiritual realities are too hard for me to understand, I become paralyzed by fear and uncertainty. Though on the surface I don't necessarily consider myself a pragmatic, I identify very strongly with Philip.

Sometimes I wonder why Jesus needed, and still needs, some pragmatists in the work of the kingdom.

True, pragmatists are good at managing the workers, tracking the expenses, implementing the details in carrying out the mission statement. In Jesus's final command to go out into all the world and make disciples, it's natural to think of Philip behind the scenes, creating an organizational chart, evaluating the most strategic uses of buildings and other physical assets, and of course balancing the budget. In the typical church today, Philip might lead the board of trustees or serve as the administrative pastor, overseeing the business of the church. And, in fact, those are the roles in which you might find most pragmatics today. Those are the areas in which they are gifted. And we do need their gifts in those areas.

However, even for these practical, down-to-earth pragmatics, there is a higher calling.

Jesus's command is for *all of us* to go into the world and make disciples. Perhaps I am splitting hairs here, but I think that if we limit pragmatics to the business of the church, we limit God's purpose for them.

At the Last Supper, Jesus seems to use Philip's request to "show us the Father" as a springboard for a much deeper explanation of God's ways. He promises that "whoever believes in me will do the works I have been doing, and they will do even greater things than these" (John 14:12).

So how can God use a pragmatic like Philip—analytical to a fault, unable to see Jesus right in front of his face? Or how can God use a backdoor pragmatic like me—calloused by hardship, with an added layer of nihilism to boot? How can people like Philip and me ever minister to others in Jesus's name?

Philip's pragmatism is a tough nut to crack. His view of reality is turned upside down by the new reality of the kingdom of God. He wrestles with it all the way to the cross.

But in the end, after seeing the resurrection of Christ, the most impractical event in all of history, Philip really gets it. He *knows* Jesus, in the fullest sense of the word—not only in his mind, but in his heart and soul.

Some time later, on the road to Gaza, Philip meets a powerful Ethiopian official who is reading scriptures about the Messiah. The official asks Philip questions, accepts the answers, and ultimately is baptized.

Think about that. Up until this time, the gospel has been spreading up through Asia Minor only. But this high-ranking Ethiopian convert opens a doorway for the gospel into the entire continent of Africa.

Philip the pragmatist has become Philip the evangelist.

He's still pragmatic, but he now can help other pragmatists in their questions and battles about faith—because he has asked those same questions and fought those same battles, and he has come out on the other side.

7

THE UBER-LOSER

HATED BY EVERYONE BUT JESUS

Imagine a loser so despicable that even other losers can't stand him. A loser among losers. Is that even possible? I didn't think so, until I came across this guy.

I tried and tried to identify with this one, to explain how his loser qualities were similar to mine, but I kept getting stuck. I couldn't quite put my finger on the problem, but finally I figured it out.

I didn't *want* to identify with him. Instead, I found myself standing among the masses, pointing my own finger of condemnation at him. Even I, a self-proclaimed loser, thought he was a bigger loser than me. His loserness was so obvious, it was out in the open for everyone to see.

It's not Judas Iscariot.

It's Matthew—the tax collector.

For grumpy taxpayers like me, and maybe you too, it's not hard to despise the tax man. Show of hands: Other than maybe his family, who loves to see him coming? Who loves the idea of an audit? By contrast, who loves *jokes* about the tax man? (My favorite: The hospital gardener discovers two doctors digging through the flower beds. "Excuse me," he says. "Have you lost something?" "No," say the doctors. "We're doing a heart transplant for an IRS agent, and we need to find a suitable stone.")

Thus far, I have had only one encounter with "the tax man." I was a recent college graduate, relatively new to the workforce. I had made a mistake on my tax forms, and I owed some money. I learned of the error in a letter from the IRS, so I called them to see if I could set up some kind of payment plan.

The woman who took my call was cold and no-nonsense, with a knack for making a person feel like the lowest slime on the slime chart, just with her vocal inflections. It was one of the most stressful conversations I have ever had. I don't even like talking on the phone to a friend, much less to someone who sounds like an adversary. But I paid off what she said I owed, and now I have a professional prepare my tax returns so that (I hope) I will never have to deal with anyone like her, ever again.

Now, I know she was just doing her job, and I'm sure she was highly qualified to do so. She didn't mean to frighten me, threaten me, or cause me any undue stress (I think). But even as scary as she was to me, she was Mother Teresa compared to the tax collectors of New Testament times.

Today's tax collectors are not on commission; they don't get a percentage of all the money they collect for the government (unless they are embezzling, of course, and we have laws to prosecute that).

But in Jesus's day the tax collector had a personal stake in the matter, and there were few laws to rein him in. He worked for the all-powerful

Roman government, and he was sworn to deliver a certain amount of tax money to Rome. If he could not collect it all from the taxpayers, he had to make up the difference, along with penalties, out of his own pocket. Also, though tax rates often were regulated by law, typically they were unpublished and unknown to the average citizen. So the tax man quoted a price and the taxpayer had to pay, even when the amount was based on personal corruption or loopholes in the system.

For the taxpayers it was a lose-lose situation, with no legal process or whistle-blower protection laws to support their complaints; and besides, to whom would they complain?

But for the tax collector, it was a legal, government-sanctioned get-rich-quick scheme. He had a great incentive to squeeze every last cent out of the taxpayers, and no incentive not to. He could extort as much money as he dared. Who would oppose him?

For Jewish taxpayers living under the occupying Roman government, it was even worse. The person who collected their taxes was often a fellow Jew and therefore a traitor, selling them out to their oppressors for personal gain. And because his whole profession was based on fleecing God's own people, he was seen as a traitor even against Yahweh himself.

A whole new level of sleaze.

For all of these reasons, the Jews hated the tax man: he was a turncoat, an extortionist, a cheat. To the Romans, he provided an important service. But to the locals, he was the lowest of the low. In fact, some of his victims probably wished they could kill him.

So why didn't they? Well, he was a representative of the Roman government. Any attempt to harm him could conceivably bring down the wrath of Rome, which had total power and authority over all of Palestine.

Not a good idea.

So the Jews responded to this unjust situation with the only sanctions available to them: social and religious shunning.

Tax collectors, like drunkards and prostitutes, were not permitted to testify in Jewish legal matters. They were not even allowed to enter the synagogue. So they could not worship God in the ways required by Jewish law.

I wonder if Matthew's life was lonely. As a tax collector, he would have been shunned, avoided, and prohibited from participating in the normal religious and social practices of the Jewish community.

On the other hand, though, his situation was a cake he baked. Apparently driven by the profit incentives of being a tax collector, Matthew chose personal profit over fellowship with Yahweh and the people of Yahweh. Between God and mammon, he chose mammon.

Sympathy for Matthew? I don't think so. After all, he had his wealth and the company of other scumbags like him. If he suffered pain due to his own ungodly choices, well, he had it coming, right?

But then Matthew meets Jesus. The Gospels tell it like this.

Matthew is sitting in his tax booth, and Jesus starts walking over (Matt. 9:9). The tax booth would have been the equivalent of your local IRS office.

I can only guess what the disciples were thinking as Jesus approached Matthew. How many times in the past had they handed over their hard-earned income to this hated traitor, knowing he was surely enriching himself with it? They must have watched with bated breath, thinking that their Messiah finally was preparing to turn the tables, right all wrongs, and give Matthew his long overdue comeuppance. How about leprosy? Yeah, Jesus—leprosy! Or maybe Jesus would call down fire and brimstone and strike him dead on the spot, sending him straight to hell.

Yes, Matthew was about to meet his destiny.

Imagine the anticipation.

And then ... imagine that anticipation turning to horror as Jesus looks at Matthew and says, "Follow me."

Follow me?! Are you *kidding* me? That's not fire-and-brimstone vengeance at all. *At all.* In fact, that's not even a rebuke. No chastisement. No demand for repentance or restitution. Nothing that could remotely be considered a condemnation.

Instead, Jesus's statement is an *invitation*—the very same invitation that he had extended to the other disciples. Surely that can't be fair.

The disciples must have been terribly frustrated by this turn of events—and perhaps even more by Matthew's reaction. The hated tax collector says nothing. He simply gets up from the tax booth and follows Jesus, leaving it all behind. Apparently, Matthew's decision is instant and final. He shows no sign of waffling.

There is no turning back.

This decision might appear to be spontaneous, even careless. But I am sure that Matthew, the shrewd profiteer, knew exactly which bridges he was burning—and how far the repercussions would reach.

Every now and then you'll hear a story about someone who builds an empire and then walks away from it all.

That's what Matthew does here.

He leaves it all behind—not only his cushy job, with all of its wealth and security, but also the safety and protection of Rome. He walks, exposed and vulnerable, into the very community of people he has cheated and betrayed. He gives up everything for one man—a controversial rabbi who doesn't even have the support of the religious leaders, let alone the political ones.

Not much protection there.

Matthew's new position is frightening to consider. He now has no one on his side—not the Romans, not the Jews. He has only Jesus.

All because Jesus said, "Follow me."

Matthew's response speaks volumes about his heart.

Immediately, he invites Jesus to come home to eat with him (v. 10). But I think this was much more than an ordinary meal. I think it was a major blowout. I believe Matthew is so sure of his decision, so thrilled that Jesus has chosen *him*, the cheat, the traitor, the loser of all losers, that he wants everyone to come over and celebrate with him, and just enjoy hanging out with Jesus.

Matthew invites all his friends—others like himself, the human debris of society—to dine with this intriguing new teacher who has called him by name. Jesus doesn't seem to mind, as he has shown a pattern of hanging out with such people throughout his whole life. The Gospels call them "sinners."

At this point, some historical context is in order. In Jesus's day, politically the Jewish people were ruled by the Romans. But spiritually they were ruled by the Jewish religious leaders, especially the "Pharisees and the teachers of the law" (Matt. 5:20). The Pharisees were a group who believed all Jews should observe the Jewish religious law as perfectly as possible, and the teachers of the law were the ones who interpreted and taught that law.

All of this might have been fine had they stuck to God's own law (and provisions for grace) as recorded in the Old Testament. But instead, over the centuries they expanded what God had said with more and more man-made requirements, until "the law" had become an impossibly burdensome code that even they themselves could not keep. Yet if anyone else failed to keep it, the Pharisees called him a "sinner"—a term commonly applied to prostitutes and tax collectors (Matt. 21:31–32).

When Jesus arrives on the scene, however, he scathingly rebukes the Pharisees' hypocrisy (see especially Matt. 23). His point is that "sinners" know they are broken and need a Savior—but the Pharisees, who are even more broken, feel no such need at all.

To the Pharisees, Matthew's celebration with other "sinners" is a disgusting event—one in which Jesus, a religious teacher himself, should have no part. But to Matthew, a wrongdoer who has just been forgiven and accepted by God, it's time to raise the roof!

The poor disciples are caught in the middle. All of their lives, they have been taught to respect the tradition of the highly learned Pharisees as if it were God's own law. So, when the Pharisees ask the disciples why Jesus is violating that tradition by partying with Matthew (Matt. 9:11), apparently they don't know what to say, because the only answer recorded in Scripture is from Jesus: "On hearing this, Jesus said, 'It is not the healthy who need a doctor, but the sick. But go and learn what this means: "I desire mercy, not sacrifice." For I have not come to call the righteous, but sinners'" (vv. 12–13).

I think the disciples' response is normal. When I was a kid, I used to return from my church's summer camp brimming with joy. At camp, I was enveloped in a Christian bubble, with youth pastors and counselors who befriended me, encouraged me, and prayed with me. There were uplifting Bible studies, dynamic chapel services, and meaningful experiences around the campfire. I always left camp feeling that I had had an encounter with God. I felt I could take on the world, telling everyone about the love of Jesus.

That usually lasted about a week. Then life pushed Jesus to the background again. I was still a Christian, but the excitement was dimmed.

This pattern serves as a metaphor for the whole Christian life. When we first meet Jesus, we often feel thrilled and excited. Then life happens—jobs, relationships, bills, disappointments, unmet goals, midlife—and the encounter fades into the background. We still are saved by his miraculous grace, but sometimes we take it for granted. And we hate to admit it, but when we see new believers all aglow from their first encounter with him, sometimes we think, *Isn't that a bit over the top? Soon they'll get over it and settle down, like me.*

For Matthew, though, the joy is fresh. For the first time, he has met Jesus. For the first time, he has received grace to cover his obvious sins. Giddy with celebration, he invites all the other lowlifes of society to come and meet Jesus too. And he is able to introduce these "sinners" to Jesus in a way that the other disciples never could.

Matthew makes a total turnaround, experiencing the thrill of acceptance and extending it to everyone around him. Yet here I am, though just another sinner saved by grace, judging Matthew and unwilling to accept him in return. Here I am, questioning Jesus silently as to whether this whole thing is really a good idea. I mean, come on. Even common sense dictates that when launching a great new ministry, the last thing you need is bad PR from adding a known sleazeball like Matthew to your staff.

Like me, the other disciples must have been stunned by Jesus's pick, and at least one of them must have been nearly enraged.

Remember Simon? As a Zealot, he would have hated two groups of people: the Romans and the Jews who sympathized or collaborated with them. But now, as the two men followed Jesus together, Simon the Zealot would have to eat, sleep, live, and work alongside Matthew the traitor, accepting him as a brother. If he could not, it would be Simon, not Matthew, who would have to go.

I suspect that Simon's choice was not an easy one.

But Jesus's call makes us all equals.

I find it ironic that while I do see myself as a loser, Matthew shows me that I have created a hierarchy among losers. And at the bottom of the totem pole, I place the tax man. I'm still on the totem pole—but I'm not as bad as he is! Somehow, though my loser qualities are open and obvious, I judge the loser qualities in certain others, like Matthew, to be worse than mine.

And the same is true for the label of "sinner." How can I—a sinner myself—look down my nose and condemn others for their sins? Yet I do it all the time. How many times have I wondered in my own heart, or even out loud, why Jesus would forgive *that* sinner?

What hypocrisy!

The 1980s and 1990s were rough times for Christian ministries in the United States. Leader after leader crashed and burned because of sin. We call it a "fall from grace"—but too often, it is actually a fall from pride, lust, or greed.

When I was growing up, my pastor's family introduced me to the sharp-witted observations of Mike Warnke, a Christian comic who spoke of how he had been a Satanist high priest in college, before his conversion. I became a huge fan of Warnke. Whenever he released a new tape (yes, it was tapes back then), I bought it. Whenever he made an appearance anywhere within driving distance, I attended it.

I even devoured his autobiography, *The Satan Seller*. I was captivated by his dramatic testimony.

And so were many others. Warnke spoke to packed houses across the country and took up huge offerings, saying the money would be used to help others still trapped in Satanism. He even appeared on such TV shows as *20/20*, *Larry King Live*, and *The Oprah Winfrey Show*.[1]

Then two reporters from a Christian magazine did some investigating. They interviewed dozens of Warnke's closest personal associates from the period in which he claimed to have been a Satanist high priest. All of these people reported that Warnke had never been anything more than a college student with a creative imagination.[2] The reporters also interviewed former employees of Warnke's ministry, who reported seeing improprieties in Warnke's financial records and personal life.[3] The reporters' claims later were corroborated by independent reporting in the secular media.[4]

I remember Warnke's recording company dropping him and offering to buy back his tapes. I remember his autobiography being reclassified as fiction.

I was devastated. I had invited non-Christian friends to Warnke's shows. I had seen some of them go forward in the altar calls.

This devastation came after I had seen other Christian leaders exposed in scandals of adultery, prostitution, and fraud. Two of them were Jimmy Swaggart and Jim Bakker. I was a sophomore at Liberty University when the Jim Bakker/PTL ministry imploded in South Carolina, and the president of Liberty, Jerry Falwell, stepped in to help clean up the mess.

And after college, I was working as a deejay when several Christian artists, whose music had touched me deeply, succumbed to drugs, sexual sin, or divorce, sometimes even saying it was "God's will."

I was young, and deeply hurt and betrayed by the actions of these leaders at the highest levels of Christianity. How could they allow themselves to fall as they did? How could they be so careless, so vulnerable, so heartbreakingly stupid? Couldn't they resist temptation when it came?

In my hurt—mixed with legalistic theology—I called for their heads. I stood behind Jesus, glaring over his shoulder at them, entertaining thoughts that they deserved not mercy but judgment.

They let me down—and I was mad.

They were *losers.* With a capital L.

Then I started thinking about how I had created a hierarchy of sin, just as the disciples did with Matthew. You know: which sins are the worst? Surely not my own.

But I know myself. I am Matthew, standing in need of forgiveness. How can I condemn other Christians who have fallen? I am just as guilty, just as prone to sin and failure as they.

So am I saying we all should ignore sin in others simply because we are vulnerable to it ourselves? No. Sin must always be addressed in the Christian community, and how to do so appropriately is a topic for another time, another book. My focus here is on my own hypocrisy: judging others as if I myself am above or beyond sin.

And now, Christians have online networks and Internet forums—new tools with which to devour each other. Professed Christians claim that "those" sinners had it coming, "those" sinners were never truly saved to begin with, "those" sinners deserve to have their wicked ways exposed. Though I have never posted such judgments, I have thought them. But Scripture teaches us to judge fellow believers in private (Matt. 18), and only for sins, not for mere quirks or opinions. Even then, such judgments should be made with great humility and fear, remembering that we too can fall: "Brothers and sisters, if someone is caught in a sin, you who live by the Spirit should restore that person gently. But watch yourselves, or you also may be tempted" (Gal. 6:1).

So it is true that Matthew is a traitor, a sellout, a cheat. He's all these things and more. He's the worst kind of sinner, despised even by other sinners.

Yet Jesus calls him to be a disciple.

I don't want Matthew to be a disciple. I want Matthew to be fried by fire from heaven.

And even since the 1980s and 1990s, I still feel that way sometimes.

The months after losing my high-school teaching job were a time of great struggle for me. I still have no idea how, after six years of great evaluations and positive feedback from students and administrators alike, I suddenly went from being seen as an asset to being seen as a liability. From my point of view, it felt like I was forced out with no reason.

So I focused my wrath on the administrator who made the final cut.

From the safety of my home, I openly questioned everything he had done, judging his actions and motivations and gossiping about him to others. I gloated over his failed attempts to revive dying programs that had flourished under my leadership. I accused him behind his back of being outside the will of God and behaving in ways beyond the love of Christ (ironically, judging his behavior while remaining blind to my own). I even threw angry tirades at God, asking why that guy still had a job when I did not.

Yet like Matthew, this man is a child of God, a disciple of Jesus Christ. Judging right and wrong is up to Jesus, and Jesus doesn't need my help.

But I need *his* help—to heal my broken, sinful heart.

When Jesus stands toe-to-toe with a reviled sinner and says, "Follow me," and the sinner follows, how will I respond? Will I dare to imagine that I am somehow above that sinner? Matthew's story is not only a story of grace and forgiveness for Matthew. It is also a call to self-examination and repentance for every other Christ-follower who would judge him.

Which brings me back to Mike Warnke. Even after all these years, even despite everything he did—the self-aggrandizement, the deception, the violation of public trust—I believe his decision to follow Christ was, on some level, as real as my own.

And somewhere, in one of his many performances, he said something that is still lodged deep in my memory.

He said, "When I stand before the throne to be judged, none of you is going to be sitting on it. We're all going to be on the same side."

That's true for Matthew, the tax man who sold out his people and his God. It's true for Mike Warnke, Jim Bakker, and all of the other prominent Christians who ever fell into sin, shaking the faith of those who trusted them. It's true for the people who took away my dream job and my PhD, leaving me with a very uncertain future.

And it's true for me, too.

8

THE BETRAYER

IS THERE A ROAD TO NO RETURN?

Once, while on vacation with my family, I saw one of those famous outdoor passion plays.

The spectacle was larger than life and thrilling to see. Against a mountainous backdrop and the vibrant colors of sunset, a set representing ancient Jerusalem sprawled across our field of vision, with a hill to the right for the dreaded crucifixion scene.

The action began with actors herding live sheep, goats, geese, and even two camels from one end of the set to the other.

Finally, the principal actors gathered onstage, with Jesus standing at the center.

We settled in to watch the final days of Jesus's life, played out in a matter of three hours.

This, like most modern passion plays, was presented in the style of an epic Cecil B. DeMille movie, circa 1950s. The male characters all spoke in the same deep baritone voice, as if no men who lived in Jesus's time ever had any other voice. Their dialogue was peppered with "thees," "thous" and "thines," as if the citizens of ancient Palestine spoke King James English. Every expression of face, voice, or body was exaggerated many times beyond how any normal person would ever look, speak, or act, even in response to extraordinary events. Subtlety was nowhere to be found.

Then there was Jesus.

He wore a robe of snowy white, noticeably several shades whiter than that of any other character, with the standard blue sash over one shoulder. No matter where he was—in a slimy fishing boat, on a dusty road, in the rugged desert—dirt evaded him. James Bond–like, this Jesus was the quintessential male, not overly chiseled like a bodybuilder, yet clearly the most confident and manly character on the set. His neatly trimmed beard was set handsomely on the lower half of his fair-skinned face. His perfect blond hair flowed just to his shoulders and fluttered in the gentle breeze, as if for a shampoo commercial. I couldn't see for sure, but I'm betting his eyes were blue. This Jesus was a man of few words, and when he did speak it was with the utmost authority.

He was always teaching, never just making small talk. He looked sincere enough but seemed to be above any show of emotion, except for one practiced look of joy when dandling a child on his knee, and another of agony when carrying a massive cross on his back.

In such depictions, in typical 1950s epic fashion, Jesus is shown as the ultimate good guy, the hero in white—adored by every woman, admired by every man.

And in typical 1950s epic fashion, if there is a hero in white, there must be a villain in black—an enemy, an antagonist, an arch-nemesis whose sole mission is to bring the hero down. Like the hero, the villain is a man of few words. But unlike the hero, the villain's diabolical nature oozes from every pore—his deep-set eyes dart to and fro like a lion in the bush, waiting for the perfect moment to pounce.

In the story of Jesus, of course, the archnemesis is Satan. But Satan, not being human, usually isn't portrayed in passion plays. So, since Satan rarely makes an appearance, the obvious character to step into the role of antagonist is Judas Iscariot.

In the passion play I saw, the Judas character, like the Jesus character, followed the stereotypic portrayal. Dressed in a black robe, or at least a robe several shades darker than the others, he was silent and furtive, always standing off to the side or lagging behind the others. Everything about him—his walk, his speech, his every expression—was stealthy and suspicious.

It is impossible to sympathize with this Judas. His evil nature is completely transparent to the audience, yet somehow undetectable to the other characters onstage.

Jesus's words have no effect on this Judas. Though he appears to be listening, he never really hears. Jesus's teachings aren't meant for him, never were. This Judas is irredeemable, beyond salvation. Yet he seems comfortable with the fate assigned to him, birthed in the bowels of hell itself: he was born to betray the Son of God. This, apparently, is his sole purpose in life, the only reason for his existence.

And everything goes as planned: he infiltrates the close circle of Jesus's disciples and earns their complete trust, even serving as their treasurer; and then, when the time is right, he sells Jesus out to the authorities.

This is how Judas is portrayed in nearly every passion play, Easter service, and motion picture ever made about the passion of Christ.

But how could the personality of Judas have been so black-and-white? After all, Jesus actually spent an entire night in prayer before choosing the Twelve (Luke 6:12). Judas Iscariot was a part of the answer to that prayer. Was he evil from birth, or did he turn so later? If so, when? And, no matter when he began to turn, how could everyone else—even Jesus, the almighty God—have been so blind to this rather prominent character flaw? Was it like Lois Lane's inability to recognize Superman when he puts on his Clark Kent glasses? The one-dimensional portrayal in the passion plays makes Judas, like all the other characters, seem more cartoonish than human, reducing the passion story to a melodrama. The only thing missing, perhaps, is Mary Magdalene tied to the railroad tracks as a speeding train comes rushing toward her.

But I doubt that the real Judas displayed any overtly sinister behavior. As Dorothy Sayers so famously stated, "[Judas] cannot have been the creeping, crawling, patently worthless villain that some simple-minded people would like to make out; that would be to cast too grave a slur upon the brains or the character of Jesus. To choose an obvious crook as one's follower, in ignorance of what he was like, would be the act of a fool; and Jesus of Nazareth was no fool."[1] In fact, Jesus went beyond trusting Judas to join the disciples; he even allowed Judas to be appointed treasurer for the group.

This raises an even more difficult issue. After praying all night, Jesus picked Judas to be one of the twelve disciples. Knowing what we now know about Judas, does that mean Jesus didn't quite get it right with Judas? I don't think so. It's not very likely the Son of God got his wires crossed in the prayer lines.

So, then, we could safely conclude that Jesus, knowing exactly what Judas would do, selected Judas to be a disciple precisely because a betrayer was needed on staff. Jesus needed someone who would turn him over to the authorities when the time was right. Jesus's prayer confirmed that Judas Iscariot was just the guy for the job.

Herein lies the real mystery.

Was Judas Iscariot predetermined to betray Jesus? Was he placed on this earth solely for the purpose of selling Jesus out? After all, as the syllogism goes: Jesus is God; God is omniscient; therefore Jesus is omniscient. At some point, Jesus had to know that Judas would betray him, so it appears safe to assume that Judas lived only to betray the Messiah and, if so, that he also stood beyond redemption.

But that doesn't ring true either. It seems to fly in the face of God's character and of Jesus's mission. Although I have no qualifications to judge such things, this smacks of injustice to me.

Another difficult question is, why did Judas do what he did? Was it his inescapable fate? Scripture says he did it because "Satan entered into him" (John 13:27). Similarly, Jesus at one point said directly to Peter, "Get behind me, Satan!" (Matt. 16:23). If both Judas and Peter experienced being taken over by Satan, then why did Peter go on to become a powerful follower of Christ, while Judas went on (as is traditionally assumed) to eternal damnation?

Why did Judas betray Jesus? Was it jealousy? Judas was not part of Jesus's inner circle, made up of Peter, James, and John. Perhaps he thought he should be.

Did he just not connect with the others? Judas was from Kerioth in Judah; he was the only disciple who was not a Galilean. Perhaps he felt subtly excluded or persecuted. Perhaps three years of feeling like an outsider was enough to provoke him.

Did he betray Jesus because of his own guilt? Scripture says that Judas, as treasurer, was stealing from the ministry (John 12:4–6).

Guilty people often act defensively and heap blame on innocent bystanders to deflect attention away from their own wrongdoing.

Or maybe, like the other disciples, he truly believed Jesus was the Messiah and just couldn't understand why Jesus wasn't setting up his earthly kingdom. Maybe he called in the authorities to force Jesus to "make his move," either in the garden (perhaps with some supernatural display of power) or in open court.

Scripture says:

> When Judas, who had betrayed him, saw that Jesus was condemned, he was seized with remorse and returned the thirty pieces of silver to the chief priests and the elders. "I have sinned," he said, "for I have betrayed innocent blood."
>
> "What is that to us?" they replied. "That's your responsibility."
>
> So Judas threw the money into the temple and left. Then he went away and hanged himself. (Matt. 27:3–5)

The strong implication is that Judas was truly shocked by Jesus's sentencing. I think Judas expected that Jesus would somehow rise up and vanquish his accusers, rather than receive a death sentence that, for reasons unknown, he chose not to fight.

This possibility is not so far-fetched. Simon the Zealot probably had similar hopes of revolution in following Jesus, and even Peter used swordplay to fight Jesus's enemies (John 18:10). Maybe, like virtually all Jews at that time, Judas fully expected that the Messiah would lead a revolution and was just trying to help it along.

Judas's true motivation for betraying Jesus is a mystery known only to Judas and to God. At any rate, when Jesus is condemned, Judas is "seized with remorse" and kills himself. And with remorse like that, surely there is hope for repentance.

Isn't there?

For some, it's a very tricky issue.

Maybe this is why we prefer the simplistic, one-dimensional interpretation of Judas: it's just easier. Digging deeper opens a tangle of theological questions that can polarize the body of Christ. And while this chapter might seem to be doing just that, it is not my intention. Instead, my purpose is to reflect on the life of Judas Iscariot, chosen personally by Jesus to be his disciple.

It is strange to think of Judas as a disciple when he is seen solely as Jesus's betrayer. The gospel writers seldom mention Judas outside of his betrayal and never mention anything positive that Judas might have done.

In a way, this makes sense: the gospel story centers on Jesus. The gospel writers couldn't possibly include everything that happened in those three years, so they focused on what mattered concerning Jesus. And what mattered concerning him with Judas was that Judas betrayed him.

But what else do we know of their relationship during the rest of Jesus's ministry on earth? Was it a purely professional relationship, with Jesus needing Judas strictly for his leadership abilities and accounting skills as treasurer for the disciples, or for some other assets not named in Scripture?

I don't think so. I can't imagine Jesus limiting his interaction with Judas to financial reports given during occasional business meetings.

Remember that Judas—and I can't repeat this enough—received a personal call from Jesus to join the disciples. When Judas first answered that call, he was not a traitor. He traveled with Jesus and observed Jesus's ministry. He watched Jesus heal cripples, cure lepers, subdue demons, and even overcome death. He saw Jesus calm a violent storm. He saw thousands flock to Jesus, and he helped distribute a miraculous meal to them from one small boy's lunch. He walked with Jesus for three years, talked and laughed with him, prayed with him, and listened to him teach. Even after Judas conspired with the religious leaders to betray Jesus, he sat with the disciples at the Last Supper as Jesus washed their feet in a silent act of service. He was just as much a recipient of grace as Peter, James, and the rest.

And I believe he was just as much a friend to Jesus as they. I believe that Judas and Jesus loved each other. After all, the Gospels say that Judas betrayed Christ—not sabotaged or tricked him, but betrayed him. Betrayal is unexpected treachery from a trusted friend. That is what makes it so painful: it is committed by someone close to you, someone into whom you have poured your heart, your life, your love.

In the movie *Braveheart,* the story of Scottish hero William Wallace, Wallace finds his army being slaughtered by the English. Frantically, he signals his reinforcements to come help him, but instead they desert the battlefield before his eyes. In desperation, he breaks away, commandeers a horse, and gives chase to the king of England.

But a knight cuts him off.

Wallace, knife in hand, overpowers the knight and rips off his helmet.

It is Robert the Bruce, Wallace's close associate and fellow freedom fighter. He has turned against Wallace to support the English.

At the moment Wallace realizes that he has been betrayed, the light drains from his eyes.

He rolls back on his haunches and lies down as if to die.

The king's guards quickly surround and arrest Wallace, who offers no resistance. The fight, the passion is gone.

This is betrayal. This is what Jesus experienced. Unlike Wallace, he never gave up, because he knew how the story would end; but even knowing that could not lessen the pain of betrayal.

Did Jesus know in advance that Judas would betray him? He certainly knew at the Last Supper because in Scripture, when the disciples ask who will betray him, Jesus says it is the one to whom he gives the bread and then gives it to Judas (John 13:21–26).

Yet at the same time, several factors here indicate that Jesus is reaching out, encouraging Judas to turn from his treacherous plan and be restored.

First, tradition says that during the Last Supper, Jesus, acting as host, seated Judas at his right—a place reserved for the guest of honor. It may be only tradition, but tradition often is based on ancient knowledge that has since been lost to us.

Second, during the Last Supper, Jesus performs an extremely intimate act of love and service by washing the feet of his disciples (vv. 3–5). Scripture says that all of the disciples were together at this time, so Jesus must have washed Judas's feet too.

Third, though Jesus announces openly to all the disciples that he will be betrayed, the subsequent dialogue between Peter, John, and Jesus appears to be more private:

After he had said this, Jesus was troubled in spirit and testified, "Very truly I tell you, one of you is going to betray me."

His disciples stared at one another, at a loss to know which of them he meant. One of them, the disciple whom Jesus loved, was reclining next to him. Simon Peter motioned to this disciple and said, "Ask him which one he means."

Leaning back against Jesus, he asked him, "Lord, who is it?"

Jesus answered, "It is the one to whom I will give this piece of bread when I have dipped it in the dish." Then, dipping the piece of bread, he gave it to Judas, the son of Simon Iscariot. As soon as Judas took the bread, Satan entered into him.

So Jesus told him, "What you are about to do, do quickly." But no one at the meal understood why Jesus said this to him. Since Judas had charge of the money, some thought Jesus was telling him to buy what was needed for the festival, or to give something to the poor. As soon as Judas had taken the bread, he went out. And it was night. (vv. 21–30)

Scripture does not reveal whether the other disciples heard Jesus say that he would give the bread to his betrayer. However, I believe they did not. The reason I believe this is that John, reclining against Jesus, asked his question in an intimate way, and I believe Jesus answered it intimately as well. It is possible that only the disciples nearest Jesus, such as Peter and John, heard Jesus's remark. I believe

Jesus kept this conversation semiprivate, so as not to alienate Judas from the group. Remember, Peter betrayed Jesus not once, but three times—yet he was restored. If Judas were to turn back to Jesus later, as Peter did, then Judas would need the other disciples for healing, forgiveness, and accountability.

Fourth, in the midst of Judas's betrayal in the garden, right after the fatal kiss that told the Romans whom to arrest, Jesus says to Judas, "Do what you came for, friend" (Matt. 26:50). Jesus calls Judas "friend." I am certain this was not a sarcastic dig to exacerbate Judas's guilt, but rather a tiny glimpse into Jesus's immense love and grace for Judas, even in midbetrayal.

Thus, in these examples—inviting Judas to the place of honor at the table, washing Judas's feet, keeping the revelation of Judas's betrayal semiprivate, and addressing Judas as "friend"—Jesus is showing grace to the one who has already sold him out.

I wonder what kind of eye contact might have occurred between Jesus and Judas that night, as Jesus washed Judas's feet, handed him the Passover bread, and received his treacherous kiss. Did Jesus extend a look of grace, communicating that the Son of Man had come to seek and save the lost (Luke 19:10)? Did Judas look away in shame?

I hope so. He handed over my Savior to be tortured and killed, so I hope he suffered crushing regret. And according to Scripture, he did. That's why he went out to an empty field and committed suicide.[2]

Sometimes I feel a macabre pleasure in imagining Judas's worthless carcass rotting in a lonely place. But then I think, how many times have I, like Judas, greeted Jesus with a symbolic kiss of betrayal? How many times have I betrayed my Savior?

Well, that's just silly: of course I've never betrayed Jesus.

Then again, I've never been in a position where I was tempted to do so. I think once in grade school I got cold feet and denied being a Christian. Except for that, I have lived pretty openly about my relationship with Jesus. Acknowledging Christ in public has never been a matter that could possibly end my life, as it was for the disciples that night.

And yet …

In the Sermon on the Mount, Jesus reminds his listeners that the law of Moses says don't murder. Now most people, throughout history, have had little trouble obeying that law. I can honestly proclaim (rather proudly, too) that I have never killed anyone. Ever.

But then Jesus closes the trap: If anyone is angry with another in his heart, he is guilty of murder. And if anyone thinks lustful thoughts, he is guilty of adultery (Matt. 5:22, 28).

This teaching blurs the line between murder and not-murder, or adultery and not-adultery.

Or betrayal and not-betrayal.

So, if you do *x* in your heart, you have betrayed Christ. But what is *x*?

It might be different things to different people. Though I am totally open about my Christian faith, I realize that there are times when I still betray Jesus.

If I keep others from seeing Jesus in me by not being Jesus to them, isn't that a form of betrayal? Yes. I betray Jesus when I refuse to show him to others, when I avoid loving the "least of these" (Matt. 25:44–45), when I fail to pick up my cross and follow him (Luke 14:27). Therefore I am just as treacherous as Judas Iscariot.

I think we all are.

Judas did not commit the unpardonable sin, and he was not

the only betrayer. Peter openly denied Christ three times, and the remaining disciples—all but John—abandoned Christ during his trial and hid while the brutal sentence was carried out. They all deserted him when he needed them most.

This too is betrayal.

So why single Judas out as the villain? Is it because his actions, unlike theirs, led to Jesus's death? Or is it because Judas killed himself before the resurrection—before Jesus could physically say, "I forgive you" and restore him to fellowship?

Does Judas's suicide disqualify him from redemption?

Does this mean there are limits to God's grace?

Asking such questions, instead of merely accepting the one-dimensional view of Judas, may stir up controversies, disrupt doctrines, and tear dogma to shreds.

It's easier to accept the "passion play" Judas and make Judas the unequivocal bad guy. Problem solved.

But the standard passion play scenarios, in replacing Jesus's true archenemy (Satan) with a human substitute, inadvertently create an impassible chasm between the sin of betrayal, which we all commit to some degree, and the saving grace of Jesus. And if Scripture truly shows Judas as an irredeemable villain, lost beyond hope, then I am beyond hope as well. I desperately need to know that God's grace is greater than all my sin—even if I, like Judas, die at the wrong time, before God has a chance to extend it properly.

I guess I am tipping my hand here by giving Judas the benefit of the doubt. I would like to think that I will see him in heaven, restored by Jesus and reconciled to the other disciples.

Perhaps this is wishful thinking on my part, and I can already hear the theological debaters spooling up to launch their standard arguments.

However, such debate misses my point.

The ugliness and severity of Judas's act only forces us to ask: Do we truly believe that God's grace is deeper even than this? Do we truly believe that forgiveness is available to all sinners who earnestly desire it? Do we truly believe the gospel?

The other disciples, betrayers all, apparently regretted their sins, found forgiveness, and were restored.

Judging from his suicide, Judas apparently regretted his sin as well. Was he forgiven and restored also?

We don't know that he was.

But we don't know that he wasn't, either.

I can't reflect on Judas without also reflecting on the power of grace. Grace and Judas are inseparably intertwined in my mind.

Strange as it sounds, only after writing about Judas did I realize just how much I needed him.

9

THE DOUBTER

YEAH, RIGHT, WHEN PIGS FLY

I remember my first knock-down, drag-out struggle with doubt. I had finished college and was working as a deejay at a radio station in northwestern Montana. The hours were terrible, and the pay was worse. For several months, I had been questioning God's wisdom and his ability to guide me in life.

Navigating the transition from student to young adult can be very intimidating, but I had big dreams. No one in my family had ever gone to college, and I wanted to be the first. So, in my final years of high school, I kept my grades up, tried to seek God's will, and made my first major effort to "let go and let God." I sought advice from spiritual mentors to help me understand my gifts and talents, researched potential career options, and spent a lot of time in prayer. I wanted to do it right—whatever that means.

When I got accepted to three colleges, I was thrilled. Instead of one open door, I had three. Again, I sought God and picked a

Christian university back East that had a very strong broadcasting program.

And God provided. Through scholarships and financial aid, I was able to go, even though the tuition for a single year was more than my family's annual income. It seemed that God was providing for me. I thought this provision was a sign that finishing college and then working in radio was his plan for me.

Four years later, armed with a bachelor's degree in broadcasting, I hit the job market and accepted an offer back home in Montana. Certain that God was leading, I was excited for what lay ahead. I was about to embark on a great adventure with God. Wherever he led me, I would follow.

For the next two years, I worked an average of six days a week from 2:00 p.m. to midnight. I worked every Saturday, and sometimes Sunday too. In addition, since I was the only unmarried person on staff, my management always scheduled me to work twelve-hour shifts on the holidays so that the rest of the staff could be with their families. I couldn't attend any social events during the evenings, weekends, or holidays—which is when such events were always scheduled. When I was working everyone else was off, and when I was off everyone else was working. My entire life revolved around that radio station.

I was horribly lonely.

Also, even with my college degree, my pay was still only minimum wage. I could barely afford food and rent. I was broke, tired, and depressed all the time.

I wasn't living; I was existing.

And my student loan payments were about to start coming due.

I told myself that all of this was preparing me for things to come, the darkness before the dawn. I just had to wait—and hope.

Eventually, though, questions began swirling inside my head. They were questions I thought Christians shouldn't ask—but I couldn't silence them: *This* is the abundant life promised in Scripture? *This* is God's will for my life? *This* is the best he can do? If so, I was sure I could have achieved it on my own—without any divine intervention at all.

Some Christians are uncomfortable discussing feelings like these. They think it may be sinful to have such feelings, much less admit to having them. But in my view, it would be just as sinful to lie and say I didn't have them.

My dreams—the bright hopes I had carried all through high school and college—began to fade into a dark nihilism.

But there was worse to come.

In northwestern Montana, autumn usually means crisp temperatures, brilliant flame-colored trees, and the scent of burning leaves and apple cider in the air—perfect weather to get outside and enjoy the season. But on this particular autumn day, I was cranky because my transmission had started doing ominous things that transmissions don't normally do. So I took my car to the shop and walked to the radio station for my regular swing shift.

It was a beautiful October afternoon.

As I began my shift, the mechanic called with an estimate.

It was $35.

I gulped. To pay it, I'd have to postpone paying some other bill and incur late fees. But I thanked God it wasn't as bad as it could have been. I sucked it up. I would find a way.

I prayed that God would show himself and that I would somehow pass this test.

As my shift progressed, though, the mechanic started calling back with new estimates as he dug deeper into the problem. As each estimate came in, I prayed it wouldn't get worse.

The estimate went to $70.

Then $125.

Then $170.

That was one-quarter of my monthly income. I could barely cover food and rent. How could I ever cover the repairs?

When my shift ended, I walked home in a daze. I needed that car. I was far away from my family, in a remote town with limited transportation options, and the car was my way home for the holidays. Nevertheless, I tried to stay positive. Surely God would take care of me.

The next day, I walked to work again. I couldn't even imagine what lay ahead.

It turned out the only reason the bill had stopped at $170 the night before was that it was closing time at the mechanic's garage. When they opened the next day, the bill rose to $260.

Then $370.

Then $700.

More than I made in a month.

At some point, superstition kicked in. It seemed that when I prayed for God's help the cost kept rising, and when I stopped praying it stopped. I truly believed this. So I stopped praying. I know—I *know*—this line of thinking is irrational and ridiculous. However, in my mind, already struggling to find God in the situation, it didn't take much to make this leap.

As the bill climbed higher and higher, my prayers gradually shifted from thankfulness that "it's not as bad as it could be" to "there's no way I can fix this."

I couldn't afford the repairs. I needed help.

As the phone calls kept coming inside the station, something else was happening outside. During those ten hours while I sat ensconced in the studio, it began to snow. Soon the city was buried in several inches, and more was coming down. The mild breeze of autumn became a winter gale, lashing the falling snowflakes sideways. The temperature plummeted below freezing.

Before my shift, it had been a mild autumn day; afterward, it was a raging winter night.

As I finished my shift, it was past midnight. I was not dressed for winter. And I had two miles to walk.

When pressure reaches the point of critical mass, it is usually due to something small, something people face every day, that puts things over the top. For me, it was my car breaking down. Since then I've had other breakdowns, in other cars. But this one was a tipping point. I went from believing God was good to believing God doesn't care. It appeared he had no intention of lifting a finger to help.

In my ten-hour shift at the radio station, questions that had been percolating silently for months were now spoken aloud in the sound-proof loneliness of that broadcast studio. My playlist included song after song that proclaimed hope in God's love, God's power, God's miracles—and each song poured more salt in the wound.

One of the songs was a beautiful old standard, "His Eye Is on the Sparrow," which affirms that God watches over each tiny sparrow, so we know he is watching over us, too.

But I didn't feel him watching over me.

As the chorus ended with, "His eye is on the sparrow, and I know he watches me." I spat out to the empty air, "That stupid bird has it better than I do."

As my heart got colder inside, the temperature dropped outside, too. Winter came with a vengeance. Before work I had dressed for a temperate fall day; after work I found myself trudging through an icy storm in clothing that was far from adequate. The wind stung my skin through the thin fabric and whipped my freezing face. The snow soaked through my sneakers. My whole body was numb.

The dark Montana night swirled around me, an apt metaphor for what was happening within.

The light went out inside me.

My mind raced with promises from Scripture: how God cares for the aforementioned sparrow, the lilies of the field, the sheep in the sheepfold, the persistent widow seeking justice. Empty promises, meaningless words. My heart, like my extremities, froze that night. God's promises no longer sank in; they merely skittered across my frozen heart and shot off into the night, like hockey pucks on ice.

C. S. Lewis experienced a crisis of faith after his wife died. He wrote that the danger he faced was not the danger of ceasing to believe in God, but the danger of starting to believe the wrong things about God. Lewis began to wonder if God was a cosmic sadist.[1]

I understood exactly how he felt.

I began to see God as dangerous—a crusty old codger with total power to crush me at will. He could do whatever he wanted with me, and I was helpless to resist.

I was at the mercy of a merciless God.

That night, walking home through the storm, I threw a challenge to the heavens: "God, if this is your will for my life, take it away. I don't want it. I can do better myself."

Again, some Christians are very uncomfortable with thoughts like these. In their discomfort, they fire off a salvo of Bible verses.

(But how does one fight doubt with Scripture when Scripture itself is in doubt?) Or they go into "counselor mode," trying to fix the doubter before God strikes him with lightning. Or they avoid the doubter altogether, shunning her as one who has fallen from grace. For these Christians, questioning God's will or plan or purpose is seen as an act of disobedience at least, and a sin at worst. What right do I, a mere creature, have to question the Creator? The clay cannot demand an answer from the potter. Ever.

On one hand, those Christians do have a point. It's silly to think that a created thing can question its Creator, like a novel rising up and critiquing its author. The Creator is not accountable to the created. When Job, in the midst of tremendous suffering, wants God to explain himself, God's response is, Who are you to question me? God never does answer Job's questions. The whole issue of suffering in Job remains a mystery.

But on the other hand, our relationship with Jesus is described as just that: a relationship. If we can't be honest with him about our doubts, then I really wouldn't call it a relationship. Even if God chooses not to answer, as in Job's case, I am hard-pressed to consider Job's questioning of God a sin.

That night, after forty-five minutes of pushing through the freezing ice and snow, I made it back to my apartment, cold, tired, and lost in spirit. I had managed to avoid frostbite or hypothermia, but I shivered in my bed well into the night.

The outcome is anticlimactic. There was no happy ending, no miracle check from heaven. Eventually I scraped together enough money to pay the mechanic, but as a result I fell so far behind on my other bills that I ended up declaring bankruptcy.

I was only twenty-three.

Throughout that winter and spring, I continued to face doubts that God is a God of love.

All these years later, I still don't know why it happened. I still don't know what good came from it. I still don't know why God seemed to let me down—at least in my eyes.

Worse yet, if that was a divine test, then I probably failed miserably. My faith was tested by fire, and it vaporized like ice. To this day, I still struggle with trusting God. When life is going well, part of me is waiting for the bottom to drop out. Surely the good times can't last.

The months that followed the loss of my job and the PhD revealed that maybe I haven't completely conquered the crisis of faith that began in northwestern Montana. With that said, I think I did gain one important thing from that horrible winter night: when a fellow Christian comes to me and expresses severe doubt, I am not intimidated. I completely understand the struggle, and it does not frighten me in the least.

Maybe I didn't pass the test with flying colors, but I did come out on the other side. I clung to God by a thread, but I didn't let go of that thread. And it was that thread, I believe, that God used to pull me up out of my time of darkness.

And now I understand what others feel when they are in it.

Doubt is common among heroes of faith. I don't think God washes his hands of those who doubt, and I don't think we should either.

In 1 Kings 19, God has just answered Elijah's prayers by sending heavenly fire to consume several hundred false prophets. But when Queen Jezebel seeks his life, he quickly forgets God's power and is tempted to give up, saying, "I have had enough, LORD. Take my life" (v. 4). Instead of judging Elijah for his short memory, however, God shows himself by providing food, rest, and eventually a "gentle whisper" (vv. 11–12).

After a long career of preaching that Jesus is the Messiah, John the Baptist is thrown in prison, where he understandably becomes discouraged and begins to doubt. He sends messengers to ask Jesus, "Are you the one who is to come, or should we expect someone else?" (Matt. 11:3). And Jesus answers him with compassion:

> Go back and report to John what you hear and see: The blind receive sight, the lame walk, those who have leprosy are cleansed, the deaf hear, the dead are raised, and the good news is proclaimed to the poor. Blessed is anyone who does not stumble on account of me. (vv. 4–6)

Jesus shows mercy toward John's doubts.

But probably the most famous doubter in the Bible is the disciple Thomas—so much so that "doubting Thomas" has become a common label for anyone who is skeptical or slow to believe something. People seldom speak of Thomas in any other context. Thomas, a pessimist and a skeptic, doubts everything. His glass is half-empty, and still leaking. His ship comes in while he's at the train station. His ladder of opportunity is placed against the wrong building. And most of all, he doubts Jesus's resurrection, the greatest miracle of all time.

I get this information from the four times Thomas speaks in Scripture. All four are in the gospel of John.

The first time is in John 11, after Thomas has been with Jesus for some time, hearing him teach and watching him minister and perform miracles. In this passage, Jesus reveals that he intends to return to Bethany to "awaken" Lazarus from death.

In response, Thomas makes a curious statement: "Let us also go, that we may die with him" (v. 16).

At first, one might think "him" is Lazarus, the only person in this story who has already died. But that doesn't make sense. Does Thomas think whatever killed Lazarus is contagious and will kill the rest of them too? I don't think so. In those days, people didn't know about germs and usually didn't speak of catching diseases from a dead body.

So to whom, then, is Thomas referring?

I think he means Jesus.

Lazarus and his sisters lived in Bethany, just outside Jerusalem. In a previous visit to Jerusalem, Jesus had been called a deceiver and a demoniac by the Jews (John 7:47; 7:20). His teachings had sparked numerous heated debates, and at least twice, mobs had picked up stones to stone him (8:59; 10:31). Scripture verifies that the religious leaders were already working on a plot to kill him (7:30–32, 44).

The disciples had witnessed all of these events except the last one, and I am sure they suspected that one as well. They knew Jesus was in grave danger in Jerusalem.

And now Jesus wanted to go back there.

"Let us also go, that we may die with him."

This statement might mean Thomas is so committed to Jesus that he is willing to die with him. However, I think it's more likely that Thomas is expressing pessimism and defeatism: *If we go back to Jerusalem, they'll kill us all. Let's go get it over with.*

Thomas's next line appears just a few chapters later, during the

Last Supper. The disciples don't understand that this is the last night Jesus will be with them, but Jesus does. He is acting very strangely, and the disciples are confused and scared.

First, Jesus kneels before each of them and performs the lowly task of washing their feet. Next, he predicts that one of his own will betray him and that Peter will deny him. Then he starts talking about leaving. He says:

> Do not let your hearts be troubled. You believe in God; believe also in me. My Father's house has many rooms; if that were not so, would I have told you that I am going there to prepare a place for you? And if I go and prepare a place for you, I will come back and take you to be with me that you also may be where I am. You know the way to the place where I am going. (14:1–4)

This statement must have frightened Thomas. Is Jesus going away forever? It sounds like he plans to leave for good, and the only way the disciples can be reunited with him is to somehow "crack the code" and figure out the *where* and the *how.*

What a mean trick!

So Thomas boldly says what everyone must have been thinking: "Lord, we don't know where you are going, so how can we know the way?"(v. 5).

Thomas lives in the real, the right-now. He's a hard-nosed realist. He needs facts, maps, tangible directions. He needs Jesus to say, "Go one mile and turn left, then go two miles and turn right at the golden mailbox…"

But Jesus—speaking of the *other* real, the heavenly, the not-yet—replies ambiguously: "I am the way and the truth and the life. No one comes to the Father except through me" (v. 6). Thomas doesn't understand; he's not yet attuned to heavenly realities.

In Thomas's two statements so far (John 11 and John 14) I see loyalty—mixed with pessimism at the horrors ahead, and grief at the thought of losing Jesus. But in his third statement, Thomas's pessimism and grief merge into doubt. The scene occurs after Jesus has been cruelly beaten, sentenced, and crucified, leaving his followers devastated; but now the other disciples claim they have seen Jesus, risen from the dead! Thomas simply cannot believe it.

> Now Thomas (also known as Didymus), one of the Twelve, was not with the disciples when Jesus came. So the other disciples told him, "We have seen the Lord!"
>
> But he said to them, "Unless I see the nail marks in his hands and put my finger where the nails were, and put my hand into his side, I will not believe." (20:24–25)

So … why was Thomas missing when Jesus first appeared to the disciples?

I think he was utterly grief stricken and just wanted to be alone. He was a practical realist who had pinned all his hopes on Jesus, and now Jesus was gone.

When I came home from England after the death of my PhD, I didn't want to be around people either. I didn't want to talk about it. I didn't even want encouragement. I just wanted to crawl under a rock and die.

I think that's what Thomas is doing here. I think he's descending into grief—grief over the loss of someone he had thought was his Messiah, his Lord and Savior. Jesus is gone; why should the disciples keep gathering without him?

So when the others say they have seen Jesus, Thomas blurts out his honest feelings, the same feelings any of us would have if a beloved friend were to be horribly executed. He says, "Unless I see the nail marks in his hands and put my finger where the nails were, and put my hand into his side, I will not believe" (v. 25).

In thoughtful Christian schools and churches, students are, and should be, allowed to wrestle with doubts about the resurrection. But when Thomas doubts the resurrection, we seem to consider him weak in faith. He had been with Jesus for three years. He had seen Jesus's miracles and accepted Jesus's deity. He even had seen Jesus raise Lazarus from the dead. Surely he should have trusted that Jesus could raise *himself* from the dead too.

But really, would you? Would I?

Thomas has a classic scientific mind, so prized in Western culture. He needs to experience everything with his senses. He has to see it, hear it, touch it, taste it, smell it. Who, when faced with outrageous claims of a resurrection, wouldn't need to see it firsthand? Call Thomas a doubter, but you can't call him gullible.

Walking home from the radio station that October night, like Thomas I decided I was through with empty promises. I needed something tangible from God. I needed divine rescue.

But there was nothing. God remained silent and hidden.

Throughout that whole terrible experience, God and I weren't on speaking terms, so I didn't pick up a Bible for weeks afterward. I just kept demanding that he show himself, and I had no intention of budging until he did.

But he never showed himself. Instead, he showed me doubting Thomas.

At first, I suspected God did this to chastise me for being so weak. But then I realized that eventually, Thomas's doubts *are* answered; eventually, Jesus *does* show himself to Thomas.

> A week later his disciples were in the house again, and Thomas was with them. Though the doors were locked, Jesus came and stood among them and said, "Peace be with you!" Then he said to Thomas, "Put your finger here; see my hands. Reach out your hand and put it into my side. Stop doubting and believe."
>
> Thomas said to him, "My Lord and my God!"
>
> Then Jesus told him, "Because you have seen me, you have believed; blessed are those who have not seen and yet have believed." (vv. 26–29)

This time, when Jesus appears, it has been a whole week since his first appearance—and what a horrible week it must have been for Thomas. I can see him brooding in the corner as the others talk excitedly about having seen Jesus. Their excitement must have been painful and confusing for him. How could it possibly be true?

Yet to his credit, Thomas is there. In the midst of his doubts, something makes him stick around—just in case.

Then, despite the locked doors, Jesus suddenly appears. And in this story, one tiny fact jumps out at me: Thomas is the only disciple mentioned by name; the other disciples are just nameless extras. This scene is between Thomas and Jesus alone.

Thomas needs to see the nail holes in Jesus's wrists, the spear gash in his side. And Jesus obliges; he is not intimidated by the earthly doubts of an earthly man.

Christians often hesitate to express doubt because other Christians respond with shock, censure, or ridicule. But Jesus is never intimidated by our doubts, no matter how silly or unacceptable they may seem to others. Instead, he meets us in the midst of them.

Jesus's meeting with Thomas is not a time of condemnation. It is not a time for Jesus to curl his lip in disgust and say, "I told you so." Instead, it is an intimate moment between God and a broken human being. It is a moment for healing.

Only God can truly heal doubt. Contrary to what we think, doubt cannot be reasoned away, because it is not a problem of the mind; it is a problem of the spirit. Like he did for Thomas, we never know when or how Jesus will step into our doubts—but he certainly will.

When we, like Thomas, are living in that "week" (or however long it takes) before Jesus reveals himself, we are living in our doubt. Christianity is not a faith that is wrapped up in a pretty little package. It often brings more questions than answers. Our society tends to despise unanswered questions and want everything nailed down. Maybe that's why we criticize Thomas's doubt. Maybe that's why, in our minds, Thomas's doubt makes him a loser.

But if Thomas is a loser simply because he doubted Jesus's resurrection, then he is in good company.

Other great Christians who have experienced serious doubt

about God include John of the Cross, Martin Luther, John Wesley, C. S. Lewis, Dietrich Bonhoeffer, and many more. It seems the most respected spiritual giants of Christian history have walked through the dark night of doubt. Their doubts became a part of their lives, making them stronger. Like them, Thomas did not sugarcoat or deny his doubts, but instead expressed them and wrestled with them. In so doing, he wrestled with God. And God met him there.

Recently I found my old Bible—the one that I owned during that dark and lonely time in northwestern Montana. In the margins next to John 20—the story of Thomas's doubt—is scribbled this quote from William Barclay: "[When] a man fights his way through his doubts to the conviction that Jesus Christ is Lord, he has attained to a certainty that the man who unthinkingly accepts things can never reach."[2]

Doubt must be explored—not ignored. Facing doubt is an exercise of faith.

And as with any other exercise, this one makes us stronger.

10

THE EGOTIST

OH LORD, IT'S HARD TO BE HUMBLE

Throughout my life, I have always sought self-worth through achievement. Achievement, I thought, brings status, and status brings value. I feared that when achieving ceased, my status would crash and my value would evaporate. So when my PhD collapsed, my sense of worth did too.

The day it happened is burned into my brain.

After flying eight thousand miles from Oregon to England and taking the train to the town where my school was located, I settled into my room and tried to get some sleep. The next morning I took a bus to the university campus, found the right building, and walked into the appointed meeting room for my oral defense with two examiners I'd never met before. I was nervous and jet-lagged, but my advisor had assured me that since my work had been meticulously reviewed and approved by him and my other (US) advisor, I could think of this final step as almost a formality—like an academic discussion among peers. I was prepared for it to be tough and thorough, but also fair and respectful.

Within minutes, I saw that it was not to be that way for me. From the moment I entered the room there was a distinct chill—an ominous lack of smiles and pleasantries. The interview had barely begun when one examiner quoted a line from my dissertation and stated, with visible agitation, "How can you say that? That is indefensible!"

With a sinking feeling, I asked, "Then why am I here?"

The examiner then took issue with the second word in my title. She was skeptical of the concept; in fact, her speech was clenched and her lip curled in disdain. And the other examiner did not contradict her.

As the interview progressed, my stomach twisted tighter and tighter. It was as if my advisors and I had been going due north for seven years, and now these two new faces were telling me I should have been headed south.

I had fully expected my work to be challenged, corrected, even picked apart. But I did not expect what happened next.

After forty-five grueling minutes of trying everything I could to correct what felt (to me) like an insurmountable bias and move the discussion in a direction that felt (to me) like a more reasoned and mutual debate based on the academic literature, the two examiners asked me to leave the room for a few agonizing moments, then called me back in and announced their decision.

My dissertation was rejected. All hope of discussion was gone. The decision was made.

Then came the last bombshell. In the final decision, I was not allowed to rewrite and resubmit my work for a PhD. The university would never grant me that degree, no matter what revisions I made or how much more work I did.

Wait—what? As my ears struggled to understand the news, my brain was already starting to weigh its far-reaching implications.

I sat in stunned silence before my two examiners, waiting for some caveat of hope. But none came. One examiner stared at me impassively. The other never made eye contact.

I already knew from my advisor that there were only three grounds for an appeal: a medical problem, an administrative error, or academic bias. The first two didn't apply. The third definitely seemed valid to me; but since both examiners were in agreement, I would have to prove they were *both* biased. (Later, when my advisor learned of the decision, he confirmed it would be almost impossible to do that.)

No matter what I said or did, I knew they would stand firm. It was their word against mine.

In that fateful room, at that fateful moment, all I wanted to do was get out. But my body, wracked by shame and humiliation, would not execute my commands. Sweating and shaking, I struggled to cram my four-hundred-page dissertation back into my brand-new briefcase—a gift from my mother and stepfather for this occasion.

My executioners, as they seemed to me, sat and watched.

Tripping and stumbling, I fled from the room.

As I slithered out of the building and down the path that led away from the university I had known and loved for seven years, I was in a stupor. Every step required a conscious act of will. Over and over, I had to remind myself to breathe. Finally, for the very last time, I made my escape through the university's ivy-covered main gate. Everyone calls it the entrance, but now it was my exit.

The irony was not lost on me.

During the short trip back to my quarters, I couldn't even look at strangers on the bus. What on earth would I do when I got back to the research center where I was staying? It was filled with other students and visiting scholars who had been cheering me on. They all knew that today was the day of my oral defense and were eagerly waiting to congratulate me when I got back.

How would I get past them?

I thought about all of my loved ones back in the United States, anxiously awaiting my phone call relating the good news. They had looked forward to this moment as long as I had. And my wife, who had labored beside me, edited my research, and contributed financially, spiritually, and emotionally toward this goal for seven long years, had planned a family celebration for the day after my return.

How could I tell them?

Then there were my colleagues at work. I was a teacher, and my boss and coworkers all valued higher education; in fact, some were pursuing advanced studies, just as I was. How could I explain my failure to them? How could I rejoice with them when they earned their degrees?

And what about all the people I would meet for the rest of my life? Never again, I realized, could I mention my doctoral studies on a résumé or job application. To do so would only raise the question, "When will you finish?"—which I could never answer without admitting that I had failed.

I had spent many years trying to earn those three little letters, at a cost of about twenty thousand dollars per letter (counting expenses for research and travel). And what did I have to show for it? No degree, no credits, no refunds, no recourse for appeal—just a huge hit on my lifetime financial balance sheet, a public brand of shame on my forehead, and a crushing wound of failure in my soul.

No, academia didn't just deliver a knockout blow; it drove a butcher's knife into my heart. And the blade was still there, buried up to the hilt. Everywhere I went, I was gushing blood from an invisible wound that couldn't be staunched.

A seismic shift had taken place in my spirit.

When I walked onto that university campus on that February day, I was a PhD candidate. One hour later, I was ... nothing.

A loser.

But in the months, and then years, following that train wreck in England, one question kept rising out of the fog: why was I so devastated by this loss, this particular injustice? In the grand scheme of things, others have suffered far worse. How insignificant was my grief next to the horrors of war or terrorism, AIDS or cancer, slavery or abuse? How could I wallow in self-pity in the face of rampant poverty, disease, and conflict around the world? Millions die daily from lack of food or water, yet I fall apart at a momentary rejection by two complete strangers.

Others have rebounded from far greater ordeals, yet I couldn't get past my pain. What was it about this unexpected event that so shattered my framework of the power and grace of God and replaced it with one based on failure, pessimism, and hopelessness? Of all the setbacks I have had, why was this one so deadly?

I am not anxious to explore the answer. Because I suspect the biggest blow was dealt not to my future, my career, or even my bank account—but to my ego.

Yes, there are many worthy reasons for earning a PhD. For example, I knew that my PhD work would strengthen my teaching, and I hoped it would advance the body of knowledge and help others within my field of study. But there are sketchier motivations too—such as the fact that "PhD" just has a nice ring to it. It sounds impressive, superior. It signifies authority and expertise. I liked that.

Yet I didn't want to become prideful. I pictured myself still being the wacky, fun-loving person that I am, who also happened to be a doctor of philosophy. It was not my intent to become an academic elitist when I began my doctoral program. In fact, I was intimidated—scared to death.

But as I pursued my studies, talking to others—especially other academics—about my research made me feel smart, important, and worthy somehow. I became an expert in my narrow area of study, and people began to notice and show respect for my knowledge. Sometimes they consulted me or asked me to speak. That was nice.

Somewhere along the line, the PhD became my source of value. It mattered. I had legitimate reasons for going after a PhD, but I also liked the idea of seeing it at the top of my résumé.

Life was not about helping others but about supporting my fragile ego and boosting my self-confidence. Yes, I did help others in various ways, but the underlying concern was how I felt about myself.

An egotist can be someone whose self-esteem is too high—or too low. The ego may be overinflated, puffed up due to constant praise for some skill that is highly valued or in demand. Or the ego may be completely deflated, requiring constant self-promotion and outside affirmation to keep it afloat. If I am an egotist, I can be at either end of the spectrum; but both ends are still about *me*. What's in it for me? How can I benefit?

Yet egotism goes against everything Jesus taught. He said his disciples must "take up their cross and follow me" (Mark 8:34).

This command defies every fleshly instinct.

Our narcissistic society worships the self; for proof, just turn on the TV. We'll sell our souls for fifteen minutes of fame. We'll subject ourselves to complete ridicule for one moment in the spotlight. The examples are all around us.

And the Christian community is not immune. Some churches live and die by an unwritten but well-established pecking order. Positions in what I call "prestige ministries" (these could be youth programs, worship teams, or anything else that is exalted in any given church) may be sought for personal attention or acclaim, not for God's glory. Committees may be joined in order to gain influence or earn accolades. Acts of compassion may be carried out to stroke the ego. People may be spiritually proud of their talent, their busyness, their biblical knowledge, or even their humility.

Don't misunderstand me. Many who serve in these areas and do these things truly are devoted to the kingdom. Everything they do is done for Christ and his glory. And God knows their hearts.

Nonetheless, throughout history God's people have struggled with the problem of pride and egotism: think of Joseph bragging about his dreams to his brothers; Moses striking the rock in prideful anger; or King David arrogantly stealing Uriah's wife, just because he could (Gen. 37:5–11; Num. 20:9–12; 2 Sam. 12:7–10).

And at least two who shared in such ego struggles were Jesus's disciples, the brothers James and John.

These two, with Peter, made up Jesus's "inner circle." James and John were the sons of Zebedee, and Jesus nicknamed them "sons of thunder," which implies they were somewhat volatile (Mark 3:17).

As I thought about James and John, I ran into a dilemma: should I write about them separately, or together? On one hand, they are very similar: They have the same overly involved mother, the same competitive nature, the same desire to "look out for number one." Further, they always appear together in their moments of weakness.

On the other hand, unlike the other disciple named James, this James and his brother John are not "bit players" in the gospel narrative. Instead, Jesus seems to choose them, along with Peter, as his closest confidants. He allows them to see things the other disciples do not see, such as the Transfiguration (Matt. 17) and the raising of Jairus's daughter from the dead (Mark 5:35–43; Luke 8:51–56). James and John were individuals, and Jesus seemed to have a powerful and unique relationship with each of them.

So I decided to give each his own chapter. But in general, keep in mind that whatever is said of James could also be said of John.

Based on the fact that James is almost always listed before John in the Gospels,[1] it appears that James was the older of the two brothers and thus likely to inherit Zebedee's fishing business. When they met Jesus, both brothers were already working on the fishing boat.

Scripture doesn't say much about the background of James and John, except that they had a mother (Matt. 20:20) and father, Zebedee, whose fishing business they joined (Matt. 4:21; Mark 1:19). They fished to make a living, but they probably had little education and even less glamor. Unlike the Alaska fishermen whose mystique has been celebrated in reality TV shows, Jewish fishermen were not celebrated in their culture. Instead of mystique, they just had "stank."

Day after day, James and John were immersed in the slime and stink of fish. They lived in the fishy oils and residue, with the smell permeating their clothes, skin, and hair, no matter how much they scrubbed. Their daily work was dirty and difficult—and the results were unpredictable: catch fish and you make it; get skunked and you don't.

Maybe that's why, in Scripture, their mother appears to want more for her sons. She is present with them as they travel with Jesus, apparently looking out for them and even advocating on their behalf. These are signs of a very loving but perhaps overly protective and indulgent mother.

In fairness to her, a couple of observations are in order. First, Jesus had been consistently teaching his disciples to pray boldly and ask for anything in his name (Matt. 7:7–11; Luke 11:5–13; John 14:13–14; 15:16). So we can hardly fault James and his mother for thinking, *Hey, he said to ask, so we're asking!*—even if they didn't yet understand the difference between selfish ambitions and godly petitions. And I'm sure James's mom wasn't alone in looking toward the future, expecting Jesus to set up a physical kingdom here on earth—in which case, practically speaking, she assumed there would be plenty of important jobs to do. So why shouldn't her brilliant, talented sons, who had given up everything to follow Jesus, get the best ones?

But she has no idea what her request really means:

> Then the mother of Zebedee's sons came to Jesus with her sons and, kneeling down, asked a favor of him.
>
> "What is it you want?" he asked.
>
> She said, "Grant that one of these two sons of mine may sit at your right and the other at your left in your kingdom."

"You don't know what you are asking," Jesus said to them. "Can you drink the cup I am going to drink?"

"We can," they answered.

Jesus said to them, "You will indeed drink from my cup, but to sit at my right or left is not for me to grant. These places belong to those for whom they have been prepared by my Father."

When the ten heard about this, they were indignant with the two brothers. (Matt. 20:20–24)

For this mom, it isn't enough that her sons have been handpicked to be among Jesus's twelve disciples. It isn't even enough that they are two-thirds of his "top three." No, her ultimate goal is to make them "Number 1" and "Number 2" in the kingdom, right next to Jesus. I get the feeling that, although she never says so, if given the opportunity she might even ask Jesus to kindly step aside from the throne itself.

For her, it's all about position and status.

From their reaction, I'm sure the other disciples nursed a similar hope. But only this mom had the courage to express it.

I have seen this kind of mom. When I directed high school drama productions, "stage moms" came with the territory. Typically, their kids had leading parts in the show, and they would throw themselves into the work of the production, doing all they could to help it succeed. However, coupled with their passion was often an unquenchable desire to be in charge, to interfere in areas that were not their responsibility, and to make their child's star shine brighter than the others, sometimes stirring up tensions and stepping on toes in the process.

As the director, I wasted a lot of time and energy putting out fires caused by these sometimes misdirected helpers.

As portrayed in Scripture, James's mother is like that. She wants only the best for her sons and she will do anything to get it, even if that means alienating the other disciples. Unlike Rebekah in the Old Testament, who schemes in secret to get the best for her favorite son, Jacob (Gen. 27:6–10), James's mother presents her request directly to God Incarnate. She doesn't care if the other disciples are hurt or angry about it. All she cares about is her kids.

Of course, Jesus's response—"You don't know what you are asking. Can you drink the cup I am going to drink?"—indicates that she has no idea of the burden she is wishing upon them.

At this point, you might wonder why I am spending so much time on James's mother, before getting around to James himself.

Allow me to close the loop. One common side effect of an ambitious mom is a strife-filled household, fueled by sibling rivalry and competitiveness. Think about it: If the mom's primary objective is to push two of her children to the top, then which of them will be first? They can't both be; there is only one "top" position.

In the gospel of Mark the story is repeated, but this time with James and John posing the question, in even more presumptuous language than that recorded in Matthew: "[W]e want you to do for us whatever we ask.... Let one of us sit at your right and the other at your left in your glory" (10:35, 37).

Maybe I am reading this wrong, but to me, their request gives off a distinct aroma—an aroma I like to call "Eau de Two Spoiled Brats."

Why is it that for humans, good enough is never good enough? Why do we care so much about status and superiority? In the scriptural account, it is not enough for James to have a high place in the family fishing business, or even a high place in Jesus's own inner circle. He wants the highest place of privilege and honor in Jesus's kingdom—the *very* highest place.

This insatiable quest reminds me of the flesh-eating plant in the musical *Little Shop of Horrors*: "More … more! Feed me, Seymour! Feed me!"

For me, I hoped that higher education would be my path to "more … more!" I thought: A high school diploma is good, but almost everyone gets that. A bachelor's degree is better, but even that is pretty common these days. So I went for a master's degree program, where I met classmates who either had achieved great things already or were sure to do so after they graduated.

To stand apart, to place myself a little higher, I had to go on for a doctorate. If I had attained that goal, what would the next status marker be? A second doctorate? Or competing in academia to become a tenured professor, dean, or chair? Would I have been happy then? The problem with ambition, especially combined with the belief that "I am only as good as my last success," is that no matter how many times you set a goal and reach it, it is never, ever *enough*.

Most of us won't admit it, but deep inside we often hold the belief, intensified by pride and performance-based legalism, that "I work hard, so I deserve ___" (you can fill in the blank). Somehow, we think God owes us something for our efforts.

That's what I see in James's request—or demand—to Jesus. James simply externalizes a belief I've always internalized: *Lord, I'll do my best to serve you, and in return you'll give me whatever I want—status, prestige, honor.*

But how do we get there? How did James come to believe he

deserved the place of privilege in God's kingdom and that Jesus was obligated to grant it? How did James come to imagine that the Lord of all must bend his will and build his kingdom around the whim of a mere disciple?

I think ambition (not necessarily a bad thing, if submitted to God) was naturally present in James's personality and aggravated by the sense of entitlement conveyed by his mother. In turn, if James was even close to normal, his natural sibling rivalry with John would have been amplified by competitiveness for parental favor.

It becomes an endless cycle: a competitive nature, common between brothers, fueled by a mother who wants—no, demands— only the best for her children. James, not wanting to disappoint his mother with second best, grows even more competitive. Then, buoyed by the constant reinforcement that he is, and thus deserves, the best, he begins to believe the universe revolves around him.

He becomes confident to a fault. He expects to get whatever he wants, even a place of honor in Jesus's kingdom. He easily forgives his own mistakes and sins; yet he views the mistakes and sins of others as gross injustices, deserving of the most stringent punishment.

An example of this last characteristic is provided in Luke's gospel. The Bible says that Jesus sends messengers ahead to prepare a Samaritan village for his arrival, but the Samaritans reject them because Jesus is headed for Jerusalem. Samaritans, descendants of "mixed marriages" between Jews and foreign colonists brought in by the Assyrians, believed in worshipping not in Jerusalem but on Mount Gerizim. Devout Jews considered them unclean "half breeds," and they in turn despised the Jews. To put it mildly, Samaritans and Jews were not the best of friends.

The Samaritan rejection is an affront to James and John.

Immediately they propose drastic action: "Lord, do you want us to call fire down from heaven to destroy them?" (Luke 9:54).

Fire from heaven? Where'd *that* come from? I think the answer lies in what had happened just a day or two earlier.

Jesus had taken James and John, along with Peter, up on a mountain to pray. But this was no ordinary prayer meeting. There was no opening hymn, no order of service. Instead, upon reaching the top of the mountain, Jesus begins to take on a heavenly form, his face brilliant as the sun, his robe white as lightning (Luke 9:28–33). Suddenly, he is joined by two long-dead figures, identified in the story as Moses and Elijah.

Remember, Elijah was the one who saw God send down fire from heaven to consume a soaking-wet sacrifice before 850 false prophets of Baal and Asherah (1 Kings 18:19–40). Perhaps this recent vision of Elijah is what inspired James and John to suggest a similar pyrotechnics display for the Samaritan village.

But somehow, James and John had come to believe that Elijah's fire from heaven consumed *people*—even though Scripture clearly says it consumed the *sacrifice*, and the false prophets were rounded up afterward and killed by Elijah rather than by God (vv. 38–40). Also, James and John seem to think a Samaritan snub is on the same level as the blasphemies of 850 false prophets; Elijah's purpose was to purge Israel of rampant idolatry and glorify God, but apparently these boys just want to punish others who have dissed their group.

Further, unlike Elijah, James and John believe that they personally have the power to call down heavenly fire: "...do you want us...?" On Mount Carmel, Elijah never even remotely took credit for the fire (v. 36). Apparently James and John feel they are capable of working this magic on their own; getting Jesus's permission is just a formality.

Did they assume that witnessing Jesus's transfiguration qualified them to be great prophets, like Elijah? They seem more like crybabies who didn't get their way.

This strong sense of entitlement, often encouraged by a competitive nature and indulgent parenting, goes hand in hand with egotism. To an egotist, it really is "all about *me*."

This attitude flies in the face of Jesus's methodology. True, he did tell his disciples, "If people do not welcome you, leave their town and shake the dust off your feet as a testimony against them" (Luke 9:5). I have seen some Christians physically do this as a rebuke against someone they believe is dishonoring them in some small way. Yet Jesus's intent is better captured by this rendering in *The Message*: "If you're not welcomed, leave town. Don't make a scene. Shrug your shoulders and move on."[2]

But James and John do not understand this concept. Instead, they stand on a mountaintop with Jesus, Moses, and Elijah and see the glory of God as very few humans ever have. At this point, they don't have a clue about who Jesus is, what his kingdom is, or what his message is all about. All they see is that they are the very closest friends of the Son of God. They must be really important. They have status.

They have arrived.

How in the world could being close to Christ ever become misconstrued as a status symbol? Status-seeking is the opposite of everything Jesus stood for. He said, "Blessed are the poor in spirit ... blessed are the meek ... blessed are the merciful" (Matt. 5:3, 5, 7). He said we must become like little children (Matt. 18:2–5; Luke

9:47–48) or humble servants (Matt. 23:11; Luke 9:48). He taught that the last shall be first, and the first last (Matt. 20:16; Mark 10:31; Luke 13:30).

But for egotists like James—or, for that matter, you and me—those teachings do not compute. In James's case, everything Jesus said and did went right over his head. James freely chose to follow Jesus, so I'm sure he must have affirmed and admired Jesus's teaching; but somewhere along the line, James's ego got in the way.

Egotists—especially spiritual egotists—love clear and tangible goals and benchmarks of achievement. Becoming a disciple is a very clear benchmark. Becoming the "top" disciple is an even clearer one.

On the other hand, becoming more like Jesus is *not* a tangible goal. There's no quantifiable checklist. No trophies or medals are awarded along the way. "Becoming more like Jesus" is so vague and squishy that it can't even be included on a job application.

But a PhD can. It's a measurable reward for one's effort, a tangible expression of value.

So in my case, maybe receiving a PhD had become more than just a goal to fulfill, a benchmark to reach. Maybe I *needed* it in order to affirm my worth. And when I lost it, I was forced to confront my greatest obstacle: my feelings about myself.

For me, education has been the ultimate ego boost. I have used degrees as a way to measure my achievements, and even to measure myself. But now, after fifteen years of advanced education, all I have are two degrees that seem to have gone bust and an empty frame where a PhD should be. And that loss has caused me to question my earlier educational achievements as well.

Now, with my ego finally ground to a pulp, I have a choice to make. I could work on resuscitating it, coddling it, stroking it, and feeding it until it grows big and strong again.

Or … I could let it die.

The Bible doesn't report a specific "aha!" moment for the egotist James. But toward the end of his life, he was a different man than the hotheaded, me-first disciple originally called by Jesus. The Bible also says that he was the first of the disciples to be martyred, beheaded by Herod Agrippa I roughly fourteen years after Jesus's death (Acts 12:1–2).

Somewhere along the way, James's ego simply died. And apparently he did nothing to revive it.

When did James's *me*-centered nature become *Christ*-centered? What was the catalyst for this change?

The Bible doesn't answer that question specifically. But between the stories about the old James and the stories about the new one, the only major event recorded in Scripture is the crucifixion and resurrection of Jesus. At the cross, everything that stroked James's ego—being called as a disciple, being elevated as one of the "top three," and even imagining himself to be a great prophet like Elijah—died with Christ. James's framework of self-worth was shattered, and there was nothing he could do to rebuild it.

Thank God!

To me, the best part of James's story—besides his triumphant transformation, over time, from a self-centered egotist to a selfless martyr for Christ—is that when Jesus called James, James was still an egotist.

Jesus knew that. And he called him anyway.

Jesus is not intimidated by our sin. Instead, he chooses to enter into it. He changes us from within. He does not hate or fear this egocentric son of thunder named James. Instead, he loves him.

It took Christ's sacrifice and resurrection to bring an egotist like James back from the brink and give him a spiritual makeover. The cross served as the dividing point between the old man and the new.

I too must allow my ego to die. For me, any status associated with being a doctoral candidate or having a PhD degree is gone—and frankly, I don't have the physical, emotional, spiritual, or financial resources ever to try again.

I am now a failed PhD. And, barring a miracle of unimaginable magnitude, I expect to be one for the rest of my life.

From this death a new journey begins, led by the resurrected Christ. There is nothing I can do to reverse what happened to me. I can only go forward. I can only let Jesus clear away the rubble and build a new reality: one that is less dependent on successes, failures, and ego—and more dependent on him.

11

THE KID

WHO INVITED THE PIPSQUEAK?

For each chapter in this book, I have identified a "loser-worthy" obstacle that appears in one of Jesus's disciples and then held it up like a mirror to see where it appears in me, too.

In the case of the disciple John, the obstacle is one that I used to share, but I can honestly say that I have conquered it completely, and with absolutely no effort at all.

I simply got old.

John's obstacle was youth, and when I hold up the mirror, I don't see that one anymore.

A few years ago, my wife and I joined a home community, sponsored by our church. One night, a member of the group innocently mentioned not having as much "life experience" as someone else. The comment was made with no ill intent and toward no one in particular. Still, my wife and I looked at each other in horrified realization: we were by far the oldest people there. We are now "the older generation."

We have become *them*.

And I was barely out of my thirties!

Well, I remember back in the day when I was young and energetic, full of vim and vigor, quick to leap over and tear down all obstacles to progress—and by "obstacles," I meant people older than me, who in my opinion were too cautious, too slow to act, too unwilling to change.

I was sure I could save the whole world—if every old fogy stick-in-the-mud would just get out of my way.

Ah, those were the days.

But now I am getting closer and closer to being that guy in the front-porch rocker, shaking his finger and yelling, "Hey, you kids! Get off of my lawn!"

When did this happen? One minute I was young, passionate, and full of fresh ideas, and the next minute I was a geezer.

In retrospect, I should have seen the warning signs. Like when I began vigorously debating my twelfth-grade students over the idea of raising the voting age from eighteen to twenty-one. (I was for it; I didn't want my well-reasoned vote canceled out by young punks who got all their news from YouTube and had, like, just registered at a "Rock the Vote" van.) Or the time I told someone I'd rather stay home and read than go out and do something fun. (I was afraid I might throw out my back.)

I even wear socks with sandals.

Yes, regrettably, I can no longer classify myself as a youth.

Shouldn't I be glad that I have overcome this loser-worthy trait?

If I identify John as a loser due to a lack of age or experience, then I myself am no longer a loser in that category, but clearly a winner.

Clearly.

So why am I not thankful for this?

Unlike in ancient cultures, in our culture today the quality of youthfulness is highly prized, even exalted. Our society worships young bodies, young minds, young hearts. Our marketers cater to young preferences; our plastic surgeons maintain young looks; our politicians court young votes. Even our churches look to the young for fresh, new ideas, and to successful youth programs as a way to get out of a rut and move toward new goals. When someone asks me why I still like working with high school and college students, I reply that it will be through the youth that new reformations will come, and I just want to be along for the ride.

Youth today are seen as visionary and progressive. They usher in new change, new values, new hope. They are the future.

It was a different story in the ancient Mediterranean world. The Spartans had an infant inspection program, and infants who failed were hurled into a ravine.[1] The Romans practiced child abandonment, enslavement, and sexual abuse.[2]

I can't find any evidence that the Jews followed such customs, but they did view children and youths as less significant than adults. Young people lacked the wisdom that comes with experience, so older adults disregarded them as having little value. Even the disciples saw them as a nuisance (Matt. 19:13).

So John, by virtue of his youth, was a loser. He was just a kid.

Although the Bible does not actually say that John is the youngest disciple, it does provide several hints to support this traditional assumption.

First, the beginning of Jesus's nickname for James and John is "sons"—which he probably would not have used if they were his age (early thirties) or older—and the second part, "of thunder," sounds more like passionate youths than seasoned older men. Second, when Jesus called James and John, their father was still young and able-bodied enough to crew a fishing boat (Matt. 4:21; Mark 1:19), which would be less likely if his sons were middle-aged or older by then. Third, as the two brothers followed Jesus to Jerusalem, apparently their mother was traveling with them and even lobbying on their behalf (Matt. 20:20–21). Such protective actions are far more likely for a mother of underage youngsters than for a mother of full-grown men. Fourth, the gospel of John, based on John's memories of Jesus, is believed to have been written about the end of the first century—so John must have been alive at that time, hardly possible if he were middle-aged when he first met Jesus.

From these scriptures, as well as strong tradition and the opinions of many scholars, I think it is safe to assume that John was very young, possibly in his midteens, when Jesus called him. If so, he may have been no older than a high-school senior when he watched Jesus die.

Chew on that.

From the start, John exhibits the hallmarks of young people everywhere: he is passionately seeking a new spirituality and a new world order, but he lacks experience and maturity. He needs strong, gentle guidance to channel his wild passions into purpose.

John's quest begins with his spiritual search. Disillusioned with the established religious structure, he is looking for something deeper, something offering personal significance and the power to change the world. Driven by these passions, he eventually finds and follows the man we call John the Baptist, an unconventional prophet who challenges the way things are (always popular with youth) and doesn't mince words. John the Baptist strongly confronts religious hypocrisy:

> But when he saw many of the Pharisees and Sadducees coming to where he was baptizing, he said to them: "You brood of vipers! Who warned you to flee from the coming wrath? Produce fruit in keeping with repentance. And do not think you can say to yourselves, 'We have Abraham as our father.' I tell you that out of these stones God can raise up children for Abraham. The ax is already at the root of the trees, and every tree that does not produce good fruit will be cut down and thrown into the fire. (Matt. 3:7–10)

The younger John is intrigued by this desert-dwelling prophet who eats bugs, wears camel-hair clothes, and proclaims that his sole purpose is to prepare the way for the Messiah (Matt. 3:1–4, 11; Luke 3:15–17; John 3:28–30). But one day, John the Baptist sees Jesus approaching and proclaims that Jesus is indeed that very one: "Look, the Lamb of God, who takes away the sin of the world!" (John 1:29).

And with the nimbleness of youth, John turns on a dime and begins following Jesus as his Messiah.

Immediately Jesus takes young John under his wing, as part of the innermost circle of disciples—Peter, James, and John. As mentioned in the chapter on James, these three are the only disciples privileged to witness such intimate signs as the Transfiguration and the raising of

Jairus's daughter from the dead. And remember, Jesus gives John and his brother James that famous nickname—"sons of thunder" (Mark 3:17). Creating a nickname for someone is a sign of special intimacy.

But despite all this, John still experiences some rough learning patches along the way.

After the Transfiguration, according to Scripture, "an argument started among the disciples as to which of them would be the greatest" (Luke 9:46). They are vying for the title of "Top Disciple." (Hey, can't you just picture the reality show for that one?)

Scripture does not name the participants in this argument, but since other scriptures portray James and John, or their mother, or both, as seeking a special position in the kingdom (Matt. 20:20–23; Mark 10:35–40), it's a pretty good bet that they are in on the debate. And the topic of who will be "first" seems to be of great concern to all of the disciples, because they keep bringing it up, despite Jesus's constant efforts to redirect them.

So, to show them what it means to be great, Jesus takes a "loser" quality—youthfulness—and makes it an asset.

He picks up a small, unimportant child and says, "For it is the one who is least among you all who is the greatest" (Luke 9:48).

Unfortunately, this profound teaching moment is completely lost on John. Instead of responding to Jesus's point, John immediately raises an unrelated issue of protocol: "Master ... we saw someone driving out demons in your name and we tried to stop him, because he is not one of us" (v. 49).

Oh, the audacity! Someone outside the twelve *chosen* disciples is doing kingdom work. Most certainly, no greater injustice was ever committed on this earth.

The disconnect between Jesus's priorities and John's is

mind-boggling: Jesus says that whoever is the least among them is the greatest, and John responds by tattling that a stranger is moving in on Jesus's turf.

Honestly, I don't think John is even listening to Jesus. Turf wars are such a concern for John that he abruptly changes the subject Jesus wants to talk about. While Jesus speaks of the least being the greatest, John wants to shut someone down simply because he is "not one of us."

So John, the youthful idealist, rejects the religious establishment of his day, joins a new anti-establishment movement, and immediately wants to make it a closed club. He turns that movement into a new set of rules that is just as exclusive and legalistic as the one he rejected.

He becomes an anti-establishment elitist. He is a big fish in the ultimate nonconformist group, and he does everything he can to make sure no one else can come in and mess it up.

Jesus corrects him—but gently: "Do not stop him … for whoever is not against you is for you" (v. 50).

Note that Jesus does not rebuke John for being a fiery young idealist. Instead, he simply redirects John's youthful energy—leading him away from criticizing people who aren't doing anything wrong in God's eyes, and back toward building the kingdom.

If John is seeking a new world order, he certainly finds it in Jesus. Jesus shows by example that in this new order, power and status will be overturned, while the qualities exhibited by little children—smallness, weakness, and humility—will lead the way.

Which brings us to John's need for meaning and purpose.

Immediately after the brief dialogue above, Jesus's messengers are rejected by a Samaritan village. So James and John, apparently thinking they are helping Jesus, offer to obliterate it for him:

> As the time approached for him to be taken up to heaven, Jesus resolutely set out for Jerusalem. And he sent messengers on ahead, who went into a Samaritan village to get things ready for him; but the people there did not welcome him, because he was heading for Jerusalem. When the disciples James and John saw this, they asked, "Lord, do you want us to call fire down from heaven to destroy them?" But Jesus turned and rebuked them. Then he and his disciples went to another village. (vv. 51–56)

As discussed in the chapter on James, I am sure James and John are thinking of a similar action taken against a crowd of false prophets by Elijah, who has just appeared with Jesus in the Transfiguration. I believe they are also thinking of Jesus's often-repeated promise that if they have faith, they can ask God for anything and it will be given to them (Matt. 7:7–11; 17:20; 21:21; Mark 11:23). I believe they are stepping out and flexing their "faith muscles." Unfortunately, like many eager but inexperienced young followers of Christ, they don't yet understand Jesus's primary agenda, which is not to destroy people but to love them and save them from sin.

So how does Jesus respond to James and John's offer to go all "Sodom and Gomorrah" on the Samaritan village?

Scripture says he turns and rebukes them (v. 55).

But he doesn't "kick them off the island." He doesn't punish them, exile them, or lock them up so they can't do further damage to his cause. Instead, he works gently with them to show them how to love.

And, over time, John gets it. He becomes perhaps Jesus's truest friend, the one who reclines against Jesus at the Last Supper (John 13:23–25), the one entrusted with the care of Jesus's mother (John 19:25–27), and the only one of the Twelve reported to have witnessed the crucifixion (John 19:26–27). The others, fearing for their lives, have fled (Matt. 26:56).

Even the writings attributed to John are unique. While the other three gospels tend to focus on factual events and details and are similar to each other in themes and wording, John's gospel gives a much more personal view of Jesus. It records many more of Jesus's actual words, including his intimate prayer for all believers (John 17). John is also credited with a total of five New Testament books (John, 1 John, 2 John, 3 John, and Revelation)—more than anyone else except Paul. His writings are especially noted for two youthful ideals: belief, which is mentioned nearly one hundred times in John's gospel; and love, which is such a deep theme in his letters that he is often called "the disciple of love."

When this rough-and-tumble teenager first began his discipleship journey, who could have predicted that?

Remember, he started out as a brash, headstrong young buck—a passionate but naive idealist, raging against the status quo, full of hot air and holier-than-thou elitism.

Every spiritual movement, especially an exciting, innovative one like Jesus's, is vulnerable to the "us vs. them" trap. You've seen it. Maybe you've done it. It starts whenever people (usually the young) take up a cause for change (usually one that rankles the establishment), seeing themselves as the solution to the problem and mobilizing other like-minded people to join in. All outsiders—even such supportive ones as the unidentified exorcist John snitched on—are considered obstacles. If they're not "in," they're "out." Case closed.

To John's keen young eye, the status quo that needs changing is the religious system of the time, a system that awards power and prestige to the corrupt elite and imposes mountains of meaningless requirements on everyone else.

Today, the status quo often targeted for change by youth is middle-class suburbia, which young people see as too self-centered, materialistic, and oblivious—or worse, apathetic—to the suffering and poverty going on around the world, or in the inner city just up the parkway.

John and today's youth are both right, and the world needs their perceptiveness. Typically, youth see existing problems better than the rest of society, and they are quick to point fingers and lay blame. The more noble ones even throw their energies into working for change. This is all well and good. And needed!

However, society isn't noted for rapid change, and the youth culture quickly gets frustrated by the slow pace.

Today, I'm no longer young. I've outgrown some of that youthful impatience.

When I was a new youth pastor, however, I succumbed to the same temptation as John. I believed the body of Christ was apathetic and out of touch. My wonderful senior pastor, older and wiser than I, shared my frustration at the overall spiritual stagnation in the body; he was working and praying for change, and God was answering.

But not fast enough for me.

So, with my merry band of teens, using Jesus as my banner, I launched a personal crusade to turn the ship around. I believed I had the only true and right vision for furthering the kingdom of God, and I was going to get it done.

Never mind that I was totally rewriting my job description, which was to mentor the church's youth into becoming kingdom people (not individualistic self-promoters, like me). Never mind that instead of seeking the mind of Christ, I was moving his agenda to the back burner and replacing it with my own.

So, since the first step in changing the status quo is identifying the obstacles to change, I identified the problem as the older generation. They didn't like new music or new activities, but preferred instead to keep funding the same old programs—programs that no one attended anymore. They revered the physical facility more than the people in it and sought to protect it from all damage or loss—even if that meant no one could actually use the church building. They sent money to missionaries, but felt no local outreach was needed. And they were open to visitors—as long as the visitors correctly guessed, and obeyed, all of the unwritten rules about where to sit, what to wear, how to act, and what to say.

And as I reflect back on that time, I can say, even as a now-old guy, that I don't think I was necessarily wrong. Many churches are indeed stagnant and stuck in the past—a legitimate problem.

What I was missing, however, was love. In my youthful vigor, I failed to see that I was dealing with broken people just like me. Focusing on my own pious agenda, I saw everything as "us vs. them," forgetting that Jesus died for "them" too.

And, I later realized, their love of the church building was more than simple territorialism. The charter members had helped to build it with their own hands. They had seen their children baptized and married there, their loved ones mourned and remembered there. Every beam, every brick held reminders of God's grace. To them, the building was an important memorial of their spiritual journey—all the Christmases and Easters, all the good times and hard times, all the celebrations and funerals.

As I did back then, other young people today often rightly accuse the church of being legalistic, hypocritical, and out of date—and then, in seeking to correct those errors, turn around and commit the same errors, or worse.

Think of a high school clique, a college fraternity, or even a street gang. In these close-knit groups, youth find status, identity, and acceptance, and the lucky few who get "in" must show loyalty and conform to expected codes of behavior.

This loyalty and conformity, however, can turn into legalistic requirements for those who are "in," and harsh judgments against those who are "out"—like John's judgments against the exorcist who wasn't in the "Jesus clique."

Again, as a staunch supporter of all things youth, I am not saying that the main strengths of the young—especially zeal for new ideals and against old ones—are wrong in themselves; rather, they are valuable qualities that are desperately needed in the body. However, as mentioned in other chapters, our strengths are often our weaknesses, so the common youthful tension between fierce loyalty *for* one thing (usually personal ideals) and fierce opposition *against* another (usually the established order) can often lead to simplistic black-and-white judgments.

So despite John's tendency to be a volatile, self-seeking egotist, like his brother James, in this chapter I am claiming that John was a loser simply because of his youth. Is that right? Does this mean that I think all youth are losers, ineffective idealists who waste their days taking meaningless potshots at the establishment? Are all kids losers simply because they are kids? Even to me, that appears to be an unfair generalization. Yet in early Palestinian society, it was largely true. Sure, kids received love, nurture, and training; but typically they were entrusted with very little leadership responsibility until they became adults.

In many ways, we still look down on kids today.

Think about it.

Would your church choose a teenager as a senior pastor, or even as an elder or deacon? Would you be comfortable with a teenager filling the pulpit? If not, why not? Youth? Inexperience? Immaturity? Those reasons might sound valid, but I have seen some teens who are far more spiritually mature than Christians three or four times their age.

None of these objections stopped Jesus from calling a teenager as a disciple—and not as a second-class "junior" disciple, either. John was on equal footing with all of the disciples, and closer to Jesus than most.

If Jesus mentored this teenager and entrusted him with the full authority of a disciple, why don't we do the same?

The truth is, God has done great things through those awkward, immature, slightly insane creatures we call youth.

In Scripture, Joel prophesies, "I will pour out my Spirit on all people. Your sons and daughters will prophesy, your old men will dream dreams, your young men will see visions" (Joel 2:28). This scripture indicates that children and youth—sons and daughters—will be full of God's spirit and will be able to see and do great things in the kingdom.

Joseph was only seventeen when he dreamed he would one day rule over his older brothers and his father (Gen. 37:2–11), something unheard of in Jewish culture. But the dream came true.

David was very young when he was anointed king and when he killed Goliath. In fact, Goliath "looked David over and saw that he was little more than a boy, glowing with health and handsome, and he despised him" (1 Sam. 17:42). Yet David was a man after God's own heart (1 Sam. 13:14).

Josiah, appointed king at the age of eight, finds the book of God's law, renews the covenant with God, and purges his kingdom of all idols and false prophets—bringing a very real, albeit temporary, spiritual revival to the land (2 Kings 23).

In the New Testament, after Paul appoints young Timothy to lead the church at Ephesus, he encourages Timothy not to let anyone "look down on you because you are young, but set an example for the believers in speech, in conduct, in love, in faith and in purity (1 Tim. 4:12). Imagine Paul advising a very young man to be an example to the older people in the church.

And even in more recent centuries, God has continued to use young people to dream big and do great things in the kingdom.

During the Great Awakening of the 1700s, George Whitefield (1714–1770) preached with unparalleled passion to tens of thousands in England and America, convicting them of sin and inspiring them to follow Christ. Few preachers in history have attracted such huge crowds or had such enormous impact. Yet Whitefield began his ministry when he was just twenty-one years old.[3]

In 1806, at Williams College in Williamstown, Massachusetts, a brief thunderstorm interrupted five college kids who had met to discuss missionary service. After seeking shelter in a haystack, they emerged from the "Haystack Prayer Meeting" with a vision so powerful that it launched the modern Protestant missionary movement.[4]

In the 1970s, at the peak of "sex, drugs, and rock and roll," a movement of young Jesus freaks flooded cities across the United States. Their fervor still reverberates throughout society and the emerging church, where young Christians are desperately (and imperfectly) trying to deconstruct old forms of worship and live out the gospel beyond denominational doctrines.

The young are masters at breaking down religious structures that we elders keep building to make ourselves more comfortable.

Cultures change and worldviews evolve, and Christianity is liquid enough to change along with them.

Christian youth really get that.

Still, the smug self-certainty of the young can really get on the nerves of us oldsters. While taking a break from my writing during a summer vacation in a remote town, I pulled my car off the road, left the motor running, and ran into a tiny convenience store to get a Diet Coke. Upon returning to my car, I heard a young lady snort, just loudly enough for me to hear, "Some people do things that really make me want to shoot them."

As I saw the heads of my two adorable wiener dogs pop up and peer out through closed windows of my car on this sunny day, I realized that she was, in fact, referring to me and the fact that I had left my dogs in the car.

Never mind that the engine and the air conditioner were still going, keeping the car's interior far cooler than the outside air. The only harm done was to my pride at being chastised by a teenage girl who had wrongly deduced that I was an animal abuser.

Such are the passionate ideals and black-and-white certitudes of youth.

However, I actually was impressed that she had the courage to speak up. People *should* speak up, because if I had been as thoughtless as she assumed I was, I could have killed my dogs.

The truth is, God uses youth to challenge us old farts, to keep us on our toes.

Were it not for Jesus's willingness to include John—young, full of faith, and ready for change—as an equal contributor to the kingdom, I believe Christianity could have become just another tired old institution, littering the pathway of human history.

12

THE SCREWUP

WHEN YOU JUST CAN'T GET IT RIGHT

As I sit in my backyard on a cool summer morning, writing this, I hear a rooster crow.

In a rural setting, that sound might be common, but my backyard is smack-dab in the middle of southeast Portland. A rooster crowing seems out of place here, amid the sounds of people shouting, stereos thumping, and sirens wailing. Keeping hens and harvesting fresh eggs has become trendy here, but keeping roosters within city limits still is prohibited (don't ask me how I know this).

Actually, having relocated to Portland from Montana, I really don't mind the sound of a rooster crowing. This particular rooster, which I can see through my back fence, is a beautiful, exotic breed, and his crow is quite soft—not like the sleep-killing shrieks one might hear on a farm. No, this rooster's crow is a pleasant sound that stirs within me a sense of nostalgia for my home state.

However, the rooster's crow will not garner the same response from everyone.

To my neighbors who have never lived in the country, a rooster's crow might stir within them a sense of agitation or annoyance.

To my two wiener dogs, it stirs within them a sense of lunch.

But to the disciple Peter, it stirred reminders of regret, betrayal, and failure.

It was through Peter that I first realized that the people in the Bible were actually losers, not spiritual giants.

This realization occurred shortly after my midnight walk home in the heart of a Montana snowstorm. On that night, I had angrily informed God that his "wonderful plan for my life" was garbage, and I no longer wanted any part of it. I haven't always felt that way, but I meant it then. And for at least three weeks afterward.

During that time, in my pride I wanted to stick to my guns, to show God a thing or two. It seemed he had led me over a cliff, and I felt helpless and angry.

I wasn't looking for a Santa Claus. I was looking for a Father who takes care of his children, not one who casts them to the wind—literally—in order to teach them something.

I had trusted him, and he had let me down.

Eventually, my perspective began to change. There was no miraculous outcome to that spiritual wasteland in northwestern Montana, no voice from heaven that made me see the error of my ways and come crawling back to God for his loving "I told you so." But over time, my pride was overtaken by the emptiness of not being in relationship with God. No matter how badly I wanted to throw in the towel, something deep within me just wouldn't, or couldn't, let him go.

It was only a matter of time before my loneliness for God became too great to bear.

There was just one little problem: I had spoken some, shall we say, pretty choice words to the Lord of the universe. These weren't the tame, sanitized curses you might hear in a Sunday morning skit about doubt. These were fairly hard-core. Even decades later, it still embarrasses me to think about what I said.

So I found myself in a horrific dilemma. Surely, there are things you just can't say to the Almighty, even in a moment of weakness, and get away with it. Could it be that the things I had said during my three-week temper tantrum had moved me beyond the grace of God?

Fearing the answer might be yes, I quickly spiraled downward. After all, doesn't the Bible frequently say that God is the potter and we are the clay, and it is not our place to question how he handles us (Jer. 18:6; Rom. 9:21)? Isaiah uses the strongest language of all:

> Woe to those who quarrel with their Maker,
>> those who are nothing but potsherds
>> among the potsherds on the ground.
> Does the clay say to the potter,
>> "What are you making?"
> Does your work say,
>> "The potter has no hands"? (45:9)

If God is the potter and I am the clay, then I, the clay, had just spent those past weeks criticizing the potter for what he was creating. I didn't like the stress he was putting me through while molding me. In fact, although I had no idea what he was doing with me, I told him in no uncertain terms that I did not like it. I let him know that I, the clay, could make me into a better whatever-it-is than he could.

If I were the potter, and my clay were spouting off like that toward me, I would crush it to dust and throw it out for good. That's what I would do.

Surely that's what God would do too.

I don't think I had a very deep understanding of grace at that time—or even of salvation. It took me a long time to understand that salvation is a work that God does in us, and it can happen over time, rather than in a single moment during which we say the right prepackaged prayer.

In some Christian circles, I still get nervous when people start telling their "salvation stories"—you know, as in, "I was saved on February 7, 2002, after dinner with my father leading me in the Sinner's Prayer. We were reading the story of Jonah. For dinner, we had spaghetti." For emphasis, the speaker might add, "It was the most important day of my life." Then, after a brief pause, he or she fires the question, like a sniper's bullet: "When did *you* get saved?"

I reply with the most detailed response I can possibly muster: "Oh, sometime between fifth grade and age thirty-one ... or so."

Clearly, some people have "salvation stories" that are much more specific than mine is. So in conversations with them, I try not to show that I feel like a very superficial and ungrateful Christian at that moment. I mean, how can a Christian *not* know the day that Jesus came into his heart and saved him from his sins? Can he even call himself a Christian if he never prayed the Sinner's Prayer?

You know that prayer. It's the one in which I repent of my sin, ask Jesus to save and forgive me, and promise to live for him—with his help, of course. In fact, the Sinner's Prayer is so well-known that there are now entire websites devoted to it—some favoring it (such as www.sinner-prayer.com), others debating its scriptural validity (such as www.sinners-prayer.info). But at some point, most people who grew up in church have prayed it.

Most of the key catchphrases are captured in this standard sample, which I constructed from countless versions I have heard over the years:

"Dear Jesus—I acknowledge that I am a sinner, and I repent of my sins. I believe that you died and rose again to save me. Please forgive me and come into my heart. I now receive you as my personal Lord and Savior. Help me to live for you. In Jesus's name, amen."

Oh, I have prayed that prayer, all right. More times than I can count. I prayed it at every youth retreat, church camp, or Christian event that gave me the opportunity. I even prayed it at the crème de la crème of places to pray it—a bona fide Billy Graham crusade!

Surely one of those prayers "took."

Unfortunately, I never felt certain—usually because there was always another Christian speaker, evangelist, or youth pastor who, perhaps seeking to get a few more altar call responses, would challenge me to look (again) at all the sin in my life. That was the hook: it got me every time. It stirred up doubt. After all, could I—the timid, chubby junior high / high school / college kid from a broken home—be sure that Jesus currently lived in my heart? My life was admittedly a mess, and nothing ever seemed different since the *last* time I had prayed the Sinner's Prayer.

But, I would think, last time I probably wasn't sincere enough. *This* time, I would be. And off I'd go to pray the prayer again.

This cycle continued in an endless loop throughout my growing-up years and even into young adulthood. Every time I was challenged to look at my life in a Christian setting, all I could see was a mess. Bad decisions, broken bridges, and wrecked relationships were strewn along my journey. It felt like everything I did was wrong, but I just couldn't break the cycle and start doing things "right." Adding to my despair was the growing realization that even the all-powerful Sinner's Prayer seemed to have no power over that cycle.

Even worse, my sins were totally boring—nothing that leads to invitations to speak about a radically transformed life. I never took drugs, never even tried anything illegal. Once a doctor prescribed codeine to help me kick an ugly case of bronchitis, but the codeine knocked me out worse than the illness, so I vowed never to take it again no matter what. And as for alcohol, well, I've never been tempted by it at all—not even fine wine, which (wine snobs, you might want to skip this part), no matter how expensive or unique, always tastes like cough syrup to me.

Diet Coke is my beverage of choice, but wrestling a Diet Coke addiction is not nearly as interesting as wrestling against actual substance abuse.

I have incurred no criminal record, served no jail time—although admittedly I have resisted seat belt laws in the past.

I was never in the military so I can't talk about my foxhole conversion.

On the face of it, my conversion story just isn't that exciting.

That doesn't mean my sins are small or insignificant. I am up to my armpits in selfishness, stupidity, and foot-in-mouth disorder. I am constantly missing the mark. I am sure I embarrass God daily. I am absolutely full of sins, just not the kinds of sins that make really dramatic salvation stories. My sin is not one great dragon, like drug addiction, but millions of tiny army ants that eat everything in their path.

Don't get me wrong. I've watched people battle drug addiction, and I would never want to walk that terrifying road. But is it wrong, crazy, or just plain weird for me to wish that I, like some people, had just one main sin on which to focus?

I'm not good at multitasking. When I face multiple "top priorities," I get overwhelmed and don't tackle any of them well. Likewise, I have so many character flaws that I can't possibly deal with them all. If only I had just one big sin to conquer, perhaps then I could clearly define the path to victory: get help, stop doing the big sin, keep from doing it for a long while, and (ta-da!) call my agent and tell her to line up the speaking engagements, because I've got a fascinating life story to tell—one that will end, obviously, with me leading *others* in that magical Sinner's Prayer.

But no, my sins and shortcomings are not dramatic or fascinating. They are tedious and crazy-making. I try desperately to overcome them, but my efforts last only a short time. Like Israel in the Old Testament, I am in a never-ending cycle: sin, repent, repeat. Any small victory in one area is offset by failure in another. I have too many plates in the air, and I seem to be dropping them all. From inside this awful vortex, in the back of my mind a question grows stronger and stronger: When is God finally going to say, *Enough!?* At what point do I finally cross the line of grace?

When I threw my temper tantrum in that Montana snowstorm, I was sure I had crossed that line. I was done with God, and I told him so. Why would he ever take me back? I was worse than the prodigal son: I had deserted my Father and blown my inheritance, many times over. There must come a time, I thought, when the

Father shakes his head and coldly announces that he has nothing left to give: "Dan, you've shot your wad. Don't let the screen door hit you on your way out."

It's chilling to realize, after rejecting God repeatedly, that you *do* want him after all—but you might have traveled to a place beyond forgiveness. Beyond grace. Beyond where God could reach you, or would even want to try.

That's where I was. And it was there that I met Peter.

If I traveled across the country and took a poll, asking typical Christians in typical churches which of the twelve disciples they relate to the most, I believe Peter would get the most votes.

Why is that?

Perhaps it is because Peter's presence fills the Gospels. Of all the disciples, he gets the most "screen time" and almost seems to be the unofficial representative for the whole group, with more questions, comments, and actions attributed to him than to any other disciple.

Those accounts, however, are not too flattering.

Let me be blunt: Peter—the best-known disciple, the one everyone has heard of, the one everyone relates to—is a screwup.

His blunders range from clumsy to clueless, with a chronic case of "foot in mouth."

I always find myself rooting for him, but it's like cheering for a cellar-dweller of a sports team: you keep hoping that maybe, just maybe, a victory might sneak up on them—but usually you're just embarrassed for them.

We seem to enjoy pointing out Peter's shortcomings. We portray him as something of an oaf, with a great big heart and a tiny little brain. In one moment, Jesus praises him for revealing profound insights—"You are the Messiah, the Son of the living God" (Matt. 16:16–17)—and in another, Jesus rebukes him for foolishly lopping off a bystander's ear (John 18:10–11).

Peter is the epitome of inconsistency. His spirit knows Jesus is the one to follow, but he just can't figure out how. He's always struggling to understand—but there's a disconnect somewhere. He just doesn't get it.

One of his first attempts is when Jesus walks on the water (Matt. 14:22–32). This event takes place just after the feeding of the five thousand. Night is coming, and Jesus urges the disciples to cross the Sea of Galilee by boat while he stays behind to dismiss the crowd and pray. But during the night, the disciples encounter a storm on the lake.

Suddenly, toward dawn, Jesus comes toward them, walking on the water. Thinking they see a ghost, the disciples are terrified; but Jesus calls out, "It is I. Don't be afraid."

And Peter, never at a loss for words—not even when staring at a miracle—gushes excitedly, "Lord, if it's you ... tell me to come to you on the water."

Now, that's *got* to be a split-second impulse. No one could plan an event like that.

Then Jesus says, "Come."

Yikes! I'm sure Peter is thinking, *What do I do now?!* To save face, he has to obey. If he doesn't, everyone will know he doesn't trust Jesus to support him.

So, in an instant, he believes. He gets out of the boat. He steps onto the surface of the water. He walks toward Jesus.

But suddenly he realizes: *This is impossible!* And his courage fails. Down he goes, beneath the angry waves, with barely enough time to utter the shortest, most desperate prayer in Scripture: "Lord, save me!"

And immediately Jesus catches him up, saying, "You of little faith ... why did you doubt?" (vv. 27–31).

Poor Peter. Even when he tries his hardest, he's still just a screwup—part of him striving, I think, to prove to everyone how spiritual he is, and how devoted to Jesus. But despite possible mixed motivations, this story shows his budding faith—faith so wild and naked that he becomes the only person in history, besides Christ, who ever walked on water.

A second example of Peter's wild but immature faith is recorded a little later:

> [Jesus asked,] "Who do you say I am?"
>
> Simon Peter answered, "You are the Messiah, the Son of the living God."
>
> Jesus replied, "Blessed are you, Simon son of Jonah, for this was not revealed to you by flesh and blood, but by my Father in heaven."...
>
> From that time on Jesus began to explain to his disciples that he must go to Jerusalem and suffer many things at the hands of the elders, the chief priests and the teachers of the law, and that he must be killed and on the third day be raised to life.
>
> Peter took him aside and began to rebuke him. "Never, Lord!" he said. "This shall never happen to you!"
>
> Jesus turned and said to Peter, "Get behind me, Satan! You are a stumbling block to me; you do

not have in mind the concerns of God, but merely
human concerns." (Matt. 16:15–17, 21–23)

Ouch! Jesus calls him "Satan"? That is *harsh*. What did Peter do
to deserve that?

He tried to prevent Jesus's death.

Peter, in his stumbling, grandiose way, is making a brave statement of undying loyalty. Yet instead of being praised, Peter is rebuked
for not understanding what God is doing. He knows Jesus is the
Messiah, but he doesn't understand that the whole mission of the
Messiah is to die for the sins of the world.

As we read this story now, two thousand years later, we have the
benefit of hindsight. We know that Jesus did die—and rise again.
And we know that it was all part of the will of God.

Peter didn't have that historical understanding, so we can't be too
hard on him.

Still, Peter's protective declaration that "this shall never happen
to you!" does sound a bit like the clay informing the potter of the big
picture. What he means is, "It won't happen to you because *I won't
let it*"—as if he could stop the will of God.

Stop it? At this point, he can't even comprehend it.

It seems that time and again, Peter's reckless words are an attempt
to show that he is on board with what God is doing. And time and
again, Jesus responds by showing that it takes more than words to
believe and understand.

A third famous example of Peter's cluelessness takes place on the
Mount of Transfiguration. Jesus, praying on the mountain, suddenly
becomes as bright as the sun and is joined by Moses and Elijah. In
this incredible once-in-a-lifetime moment, Peter—overcome by fear

and confusion—falls all over himself to respond appropriately. And what does he come up with?

He blurts out an offer to build shelters for the heavenly visitors (Matt. 17:4; Mark 9:5; Luke 9:33).

On the surface, I can see Peter's servant heart at work. The word *shelter* here may imply a holy tabernacle, similar to the one created for God's own dwelling in the Old Testament. Peter wants to honor these important visitors by providing accommodations suitable for them. And yet, with his awkward attempt to "manage" this supernatural event, Peter is so far off target that God actually has to interrupt him to deliver the main message: "While [Peter] was still speaking, a bright cloud covered them, and a voice from the cloud said, 'This is my Son, whom I love; with him I am well pleased. Listen to him!'" (Matt. 17:5).

That's Peter. He doesn't know what to do, so he starts babbling. And he goes down in history as the person who tried to "talk over" God. Again, he misses the mark.

And finally, there's the night of the Last Supper—a night so traumatic and confusing that Peter screws up not once but four times, each time worse than the last.

On that night, after dinner Jesus takes a towel and basin and prepares to wash the disciples' feet (John 13:1–9). In ancient Palestine, when people walked everywhere and few roads were paved, footwashing was a needed service and a good host would provide it to show honor to his guests. However, since it was also a dirty, menial job, the host usually ordered a servant to do it. Thus, in washing the disciples' feet, Jesus is saying, "Love each other with radical humility—like this."

But for Peter, the sight of the Messiah performing such a demeaning act is too much to bear.

So he lets loose with Screwup #1 of Jesus's last night on earth: "No ... you shall never wash my feet" (v. 8).

Maybe Peter assumed the other disciples would jump in and forbid Jesus to wash their feet too. (Hadn't they learned by now that no one ever could stop Jesus from doing anything he had decided to do?) Or maybe he thought Jesus would nod approvingly and swap places, letting Peter wash his feet instead.

But once again, I think Peter is blindsided by Jesus's response: "Unless I wash you, you have no part with me."

Now the pendulum swings the other way. A light bulb seems to have come on inside Peter's head. He's starting to understand that Jesus is teaching a spiritual lesson, but he can't quite grasp what it is. Maybe, he reasons, it's all about being clean. So once again, he overshoots the runway and comes out with, "Then, Lord ... not just my feet but my hands and my head as well!" (v. 9).

Why does Peter say this? Maybe he's trying to impress everyone with how spiritual he is, in order to move up another notch or two in the pecking order. Or maybe he's really trying to understand, but he's just too dense to get the part about imitating Jesus's radical example of servanthood. Whichever way we spin it, either interpretation does not look good for Peter.

Jesus responds by returning to the main point:

> Jesus answered, "Those who have had a bath need only to wash their feet; their whole body is clean. And you are clean, though not every one of you."

For he knew who was going to betray him, and that was why he said not every one was clean.

When he had finished washing their feet, he put on his clothes and returned to his place. "Do you understand what I have done for you?" he asked them. "You call me 'Teacher' and 'Lord,' and rightly so, for that is what I am. Now that I, your Lord and Teacher, have washed your feet, you also should wash one another's feet. I have set you an example that you should do as I have done for you. Very truly I tell you, no servant is greater than his master, nor is a messenger greater than the one who sent him. Now that you know these things, you will be blessed if you do them. (vv. 10–17)

Jesus then announces that one of the disciples will betray him, and Judas suddenly leaves the room. All the elements are aligning for Jesus's crucifixion. So Jesus says his good-byes: "My children, I will be with you only a little longer. You will look for me, and just as I told the Jews, so I tell you now: Where I am going, you cannot come" (v. 33).

Of course Peter, like the other disciples, is less concerned about Jesus's dramatic example of love through foot washing and more concerned about where Jesus is going. It seems they all are starting to guess that Jesus is speaking of his own impending death.

Whatever the case, at this point Peter makes Last Night Screwup #2: "Lord, why can't I follow you now? I will lay down my life for you" (v. 37). Again, I can't shake the feeling that, either consciously or subconsciously, Peter might be looking for a way to make a grand gesture—something that will truly display the depths of his devotion.

However, this time Jesus's response not only deflates Peter's declaration of unending love but also cuts through the shallow exterior and deep into Peter's heart: "Will you really lay down your life for me? Very truly I tell you, before the rooster crows, you will disown me three times!" (v. 38).

For once, Peter is silent. He slinks into the background and contributes no more reported statements or actions for the rest of the meal—in fact, not until well after the meal is over. Rather than affirming Peter's proclamation of loyalty, Jesus predicts the opposite: Peter will deny him. Not once, but three times. And Jesus says this in front of everyone.

I'm sure Peter is stunned. Does he feel humiliated at Jesus's lack of faith in his loyalty? Or scared and confused, trying to imagine how such a denial ever could happen? Or ashamed, knowing that, at its core, Jesus's assessment of him is true? Perhaps he feels all of these things. Whatever the case, Jesus's words cut to the quick. This is perhaps the only recorded incident in which Peter is rendered speechless. In fact, the next time he speaks, it is to utter the very words of denial that Jesus predicted.

But I'm getting ahead of myself.

Peter's next screwup—Last Night Screwup #3—is not with words but with actions, and once again he's trying to save Jesus. This time, Jesus has taken his disciples to a favorite garden, and Judas, knowing the place, leads an armed mob there to arrest Jesus (John 18:1–3). But Peter still doesn't get it. He takes a sword to someone—someone unthreatening, not an authority but merely a servant—and slices off his ear. Not much courage required there.

So again Peter misses the point, and again he is rebuked: "Jesus commanded Peter, 'Put your sword away! Shall I not drink the cup the Father has given me?'" (v. 11). Jesus then heals the servant's ear (Luke 22:51).

But Peter's most humiliating screwup—Last Night Screwup #4—is still to come.

We all know the story. Jesus is taken to the home of the high priest for questioning, and Peter waits outside, warming himself by the fire. Three times, he is asked if he is one of Jesus's associates. And three times, he vehemently denies it (Matt. 26:69–74).

He has just fulfilled Jesus's prediction.

And he doesn't even realize it—until a rooster crows (Matt. 26:74), revealing his greatest failure yet.

He wants to follow Jesus, but he's so afraid for his own life that he just can't do it.

He betrays Jesus three times. Even Judas Iscariot, considered the worst traitor of all, only did it once.

Peter is given the perfect opportunity to shine—really shine. However, as always, he botches it. Instead of being immortalized in the Gospels as a stellar example of commitment unto death, he is forever caricatured in sermons around the world as a complete and total screwup.

This is exactly the point where I first connected intimately with Peter. As I related at the beginning of this chapter, in anger and despair I had said some choice things to God, things that to me were on the same level as betrayal. I had booted God out the door and told him never to come back.

Three weeks later, I was *really* hoping he would come back. But I was certain I had crossed the line. I told God to take his toys and go home. Surely I had committed the "unpardonable sin."

But God, who of course had never left, reminded me of Peter's three-time betrayal of the Son of God. And it wasn't just a betrayal of the *Son* of God. Jesus *was* God.

Peter betrayed ... *God.*

Judas betrayed God once, and we forever curse him.

Peter betrayed God *three times.*

What's the difference between Peter and Judas?

In simple terms, Judas takes the matter of his guilt into his own hands and kills himself. But Peter, despite his guilt and shame, sticks around and goes fishing. He returns to the place he knows best: his fishing boat, on the Sea of Galilee. And while he is there, the resurrected Jesus appears:

> Early in the morning, Jesus stood on the shore, but the disciples did not realize that it was Jesus.
>
> He called out to them, "Friends, haven't you any fish?"
>
> "No," they answered.
>
> He said, "Throw your net on the right side of the boat and you will find some." When they did, they were unable to haul the net in because of the large number of fish. (John 21:4–6)

So Jesus steps back into Peter's messed-up life and helps him with his fishing. I'm sure Jesus is remembering his early promise to Peter: "Come, follow me ... and I will send you out to fish for people" (Mark 1:17).

But Peter doesn't recognize Jesus, until John exclaims, "It is the Lord!" (John 21:7).

Does Peter shrink from Jesus, ashamed of his dramatic denial of his Lord? That's what Judas did.

But not Peter. Instead, he jumps into the water and heads *toward* Jesus (John 21:7).

Immediately Jesus begins his campaign of reconciliation. After serving a breakfast of bread and fish, roasted over an open fire (vv. 9–13), he turns to Peter and asks, three times, "Simon son of John, do you love me?" (vv. 15–17).

Three times, though troubled inside (v. 17), Peter answers "yes"—once for each denial.

Jesus is giving Peter a do-over.

And three times, Jesus replies, "Feed my sheep" (vv. 15–17).

Jesus then predicts Peter's death: "'Very truly I tell you ... when you are old you will stretch out your hands, and someone else will dress you and lead you where you do not want to go.' Jesus said this to indicate the kind of death by which Peter would glorify God" (vv. 18–19).

Finally, Jesus repeats the familiar command: "Follow me!'" (v. 19).

Jesus goes back to basics, back to the beginning, back to the words he spoke to Peter when they first met. Even after Peter's public betrayal—perhaps the most painful thing one person can do to another—Jesus still wants Peter back.

Peter is such a washout: long on intentions but short on substance, great at pompous declarations but pathetic at follow-through. Yet despite all of his failures, the last one being the most colossal, Jesus seeks him out with words of restoration.

And speaking of restoration, I believe that if Judas still had been alive, Jesus would have sought him out for restoration as well. I believe that with all of my heart.

Through the ugliness of Peter's three denials, I finally discovered what grace really means. Through Peter's multiple misadventures, I finally grasped that *nothing* can separate me from the love of God (Rom. 8:38–39). And through Peter's utter humiliation, I finally understood that God truly does seek out failures.

And screwups.

And losers.

Not only does God seek out losers, but he chooses to use them despite their countless embarrassing flaws and their endless ongoing sins—even the really nasty, intentional, one-hundred-percent selfish sins, repeated again and again.

And that's not the end of Peter's story.

His denials of Christ are provoked by fear, at a terrifying time when Jesus's enemies are preparing to execute the Savior on whom Peter has pinned all his hopes. In those circumstances, who would not be afraid? Yet within weeks Peter, arrested for healing a lame man, confronts those very same enemies without any fear at all:

> Then Peter, filled with the Holy Spirit, said to them: "Rulers and elders of the people! If we are being called to account today for an act of kindness shown to a man who was lame and are being asked how he was healed, then know this, you and all the people of Israel: It is by the name of Jesus Christ of Nazareth, whom you crucified but whom God raised from the dead, that this man stands before you healed. Jesus is 'the stone you builders rejected,

which has become the cornerstone.' Salvation is found in no one else, for there is no other name under heaven given to mankind by which we must be saved." (Acts 4:8–12)

Peter is changed, by Jesus's reconciliation and by the Holy Spirit, from a frightened fisherman to a powerful evangelist with little fear of public opinion, imprisonment, or death.[1]

Yet even after all this, sometimes he still blows it.

A short time later, trying to get Peter to accept Gentile believers, God tells him in a vision to eat foods considered unclean under Jewish law. But does Peter say, "Oh, I get it! Accepting non-Jewish food is a symbol of accepting non-Jewish people"? No, he does not. Instead, he replies in his classic bombastic style, "Surely not, Lord! ... I have never eaten anything impure or unclean" (Acts 10:14).

Peter is still a screwup, but a changed one. He has had to learn grace in the most painful, humiliating ways. However, to all humanity—and particularly to me, this self-proclaimed loser two thousand years later—he is a picture of the grace, forgiveness, and redeeming love of our crucified Lord.

My neighbor's rooster crows again in the early morning air, reminding me of my home in Montana. But revisiting a screwup like Peter reminds me of another home: a heavenly place of security. A place of forgiveness. A new identity in the resurrected Christ.

I'll bet that at some later point in Peter's life, after being reconciled to Jesus by the Sea of Galilee, he too heard a rooster crow again. But this time, I'll bet it reminded him not of that awful night of guilt and condemnation in the earthly Jerusalem but of his future home of grace and forgiveness in the heavenly one.

I'll bet it reminded him of his Redeemer, who conquered sin and death for all the losers who ever lived.

All the losers like you.

And me.

13

THE GREATEST LOSER OF ALL
NO ONE DESERVES THE TITLE MORE

As I write this, my district is just finishing an election cycle in the strange world of politics. For weeks, we have been bombarded to death by political ads that I'm sure were written by fourth graders. It is disconcerting to hear our future leaders engage in public discourse that comes straight from the playground:

> Candidate A: "My opponent wants to make you poor."
> Candidate B: "My opponent wants to kill old people."
> Candidate A: "Well, um, my opponent did something really, really, really bad a long time ago."
> Candidate B: "Oh, yeah?! My opponent is a dork."
> Candidate A: "Nuh-uh."
> Candidate B: "Yuh-huh."

Candidate A: "Wull, wull, my opponent once kicked a puppy!"
Candidate B: "Did not!"
Candidate A: "Did so!"
Candidate B: "Not!"
Candidate A: "So!"
Candidate B: "Poopy-head!"

And to think that one of these children is now actually the mayor, the governor, the what-have-you, making crucial decisions on my behalf.

All I remember from this last election cycle—once the political ads were replaced on TV and radio by other meaningless drivel—was that after each election, I need to go read a book or something to try to get my IQ back up to acceptable levels.

The truth is, I would never attempt to run for political office. I have too many quirks, too much baggage, too many skeletons in my closet. Not enough to land me in prison, but enough to utterly humiliate me. If I ran for office, the best I would be able to say is, "My opponent probably is just as screwed up as I am!"

Not very inspiring, I know, but true.

Elections, whether local or national, and this last one in particular, made me realize one important truth about humanity: we're broken. Not only that, but the more we attempt to point out the brokenness in others, the more our own brokenness emerges from behind the masks we create to hide it. Each of us has embarrassments, sins, and weaknesses that are best kept hidden.

In truth, no one is qualified to be president, governor, or whatever. There isn't a person alive who couldn't be embarrassed to death by a determined journalist. We have all done things that would bring shame to ourselves and our loved ones. We screw up more than we succeed. We lose more than we win. We are broken—all of us.

So yes, I am a loser, but in the last election I was comforted by the fact that I am not alone. I am surrounded by a multitude of losers, and I don't mean just those who did not get elected. We are all losers, every one of us. This common element unites all of humanity.

Which brings me to the final loser. I know, there were twelve original disciples; and if you are keeping a running count, you know I hit that magic number with Peter in the last chapter. So who's left? Is it Matthias, the disciple chosen to replace Judas Iscariot after he hanged himself? If so, then I should have covered him in the chapter on the lesser-known disciples, since we know very little about him. Or could it be Paul? His aggressive temperament and murderous background easily qualify him as a classic loser. Though not officially one of the Twelve, he did become one of the most passionate Christ-followers in all of Scripture.

Then again, the loser I have in mind isn't a disciple either; in fact, he is a teacher. Some might be offended to hear him called a loser. Still, by society's standards—in ancient Palestine as well as in twenty-first-century America—he fits the definition perfectly.

It's Jesus, of course.

At first, it may seem blasphemous to call Jesus a loser. But think about it.

His entire life is filled with scandal and suspicion. In the eyes of society, he is born a bastard and dies a criminal, and in between he is seen as everything from a rabble-rouser to a madman. His career skills, consisting mostly of basic carpentry, are nothing to write home about. He is poor and homeless, wandering the countryside with only a ragtag band of social rejects to accompany him. He is confrontational, challenging the established culture even as it openly opposes him.

And worst of all, his teachings are crazy, even contradictory, flying in the face of all conventional wisdom:

- "Love your enemies, do good to those who hate you." (Luke 6:27)
- "Do not suppose that I have come to bring peace to the earth. I did not come to bring peace, but a sword." (Matt. 10:34)
- "Destroy this temple, and I will raise it again in three days." (John 2:19)
- "Let the dead bury their own dead." (Luke 9:60)
- "For my flesh is real food and my blood is real drink." (John 6:55)
- "Blessed are you when people insult you, persecute you and falsely say all kinds of evil against you because of me." (Matt. 5:11)
- "If anyone comes to me and does not hate father and mother, wife and children, brothers and sisters—yes, even their own life—such a person cannot be my disciple." (Luke 14:26)

This loser claims to be the fulfillment of ancient prophecy. He claims to be God—the same I AM as the voice from the burning bush to Moses (Exod. 3:14; John 8:58). He even claims to have authority to forgive sins (Matt. 9:6; Mark 2:10; Luke 5:24)—an authority reserved only for Yahweh. And he attracts huge crowds wherever he goes.

Today, he might be equated with charismatic but dangerous cult leaders like David Koresh, Jim Jones, or even Charles Manson. Those who left everything to follow him would be considered insane. Even Christians might view him with suspicion and ostracize him.

Like synagogues then, churches today would be very uncomfortable turning over their pulpits to anyone as radical as Jesus. If someone like him came to town, saying what he said and doing what he did, would you honestly abandon everything—your job, your schooling, your family—to follow this nut job? If you have teenagers, would you let them do so?

Look how the established church treats newcomers who may have a radical but legitimate message for us. Just as in Jesus's time, we are quick to label them troublemakers and crucify them, at least with words if not with nails. (Ever notice that we say we admire radical faith—but whenever people start a movement we distrust, we say they are *too* radical?) And Jesus was radical by any measure. He was a thirty-three-year-old man with no home, no money, and no status—nothing but a crazy, self-proclaimed mission from God.

For all of these reasons, I contend that Jesus was indeed a loser. And if "loser" means, in the most literal sense, one who has lost something, then Jesus qualifies even more. Paul writes that Jesus "made himself nothing by taking the very nature of a servant, being made in human likeness" (Phil. 2:7). I believe that Paul's label for Jesus ("servant") is similar to mine ("loser"). Both labels indicate someone of low position, held in low regard by others. No one seeking status and prestige would want to be called either one.

Yet all his life, by choice, Jesus is identified with losers—from his (seemingly) illegitimate birth to his (seemingly) criminal death. From the start, he is surrounded by scandal. Angels announce to

Mary and Joseph that his conception is through the Holy Spirit (Matt. 1:18–24; Luke 1:26–38), but to everyone else, Jesus is just an illegitimate child—a bastard. And I can honestly say that I have never heard that word used to enhance credibility.

Even Joseph, before being reassured by an angel that Mary's pregnancy is of God, at first tries to abandon Mary as delicately as possible, thinking she has been promiscuous. Today, bearing a child out of wedlock isn't unusual—in fact, it's barely even frowned upon. But in ancient Palestine, doing so could bring down a woman's whole family. It was a permanent stain on the family line and on the child himself, throughout his life and even after his death. In the law of Moses, a bastard and his descendants—down to the *tenth generation*—were banned from entering the temple of the Lord (Deut. 23:2). Various translations of that verse refer to a person "of illegitimate birth" (NASB) or "born of an illicit union" (NRSV). But the Hebrew word is *mamzer*—literally, "bastard."

This is the scandal of Jesus's birth. Remember, unlike Mary and Joseph and the shepherds, the locals in Nazareth do not receive angelic explanations to fill in the gaps. They see only a pregnant girl with no husband. The law of Moses required complete shunning of any child born in that way. So Jesus begins his life in a cloud of shame and is followed by plenty of snide remarks, I am sure, for the rest of his life.

And then there's the location. Why Bethlehem? Why a stable? Well, the Roman government has decreed that everyone must travel to the city of his ancestry for a census, so that the entire population can be counted and taxed. And Joseph's family comes from Bethlehem, a tiny villa with inadequate lodging for such an influx. So, although the rich and powerful might have been able to wield their influence and find lodging, Mary and Joseph cannot. Instead, they get the leftovers.

So God himself is born in a feeding trough, surrounded by livestock—and manure. I am sure it was not the clean, cozy venue depicted in our tabletop nativity scenes, with fluffy lambs and cooing doves resting in the soft glow of a well-swept stable.

Further, Jesus's birth is proclaimed with great fanfare, by a glorious multitude of angels—but this happens far outside of town. To *shepherds*. Lowly, smelly range workers, without honor or respect. Back then, people who saw shepherds coming toward them in the street would cross to the other side to avoid being contaminated by the stench.

Yet God chooses shepherds to deliver the news of the greatest supernatural event in history.

Today, that would be like an extraterrestrial visitor choosing "hicks from the sticks" to get the word out. Who would believe those folks? Who would listen?

Wouldn't God have been wiser to send that heavenly angel choir to Jerusalem—to the rulers, the elites, the intelligentsia? Wouldn't the message have been more credible?

And what about Jesus himself? Sometimes we imagine that Jesus spent his first few years nestled safely in his mother's arms, with the whole world—monarchs, diplomats, priests, and commoners—marching by in homage, offering priceless gifts and proclaiming him king. We imagine that Baby Jesus and Toddler Jesus always knew exactly what was going on, who these people were, and what it all meant. He never cried, never acted silly, never made a mess, never embarrassed his parents.

But in actuality, his early years are filled with rejection and danger. Not only is he an illegitimate social misfit from birth, but he is also hunted for his life. King Herod, believing he must protect his throne from this newborn king, determines to find and kill Jesus, whose family flees to Egypt for safety (Matt. 2:13–15). So Jesus's early years are spent as a foreigner, an alien, an outlier—until his family moves back home to Nazareth, a sleepy map-speck that is despised and ridiculed by Jews from fancier places. (Today we might call it the "armpit of the nation," as shown by Nathanael's sarcastic put-down of it in an earlier chapter.)

Scripture is quiet about the boyhood and youth of Jesus, but at about age thirty, he reappears on the public landscape to begin his ministry.

Immediately he gets everyone's attention. But they don't all like what they see. He is unorthodox and revolutionary, upending centuries of well-crafted religious tradition and theology, infuriating the establishment while simultaneously intriguing and confusing everyone else. Sometimes the crowds are amazed and delighted by his upside-down logic. Yet other times, they are so offended by his radical teachings that they desert him in droves, never to return (John 6:66).

And the religious leaders hate him the most. They consider him a mad demoniac and a blasphemer (John 10:20, 33); their sole purpose is to entrap and discredit him by tossing him loaded questions on Jewish law. Even the exceptions—like Nicodemus, a Jewish council member who visits Jesus by night, and Joseph of Arimathea, a wealthy man who later donates a tomb for Jesus's burial—follow Jesus secretly (John 3:2; 19:38) for fear of rejection by other Jews. Jesus fascinates them, but not enough to bring their loyalty out of the closet.

And the feeling is mutual. For the religious leaders as a group, Jesus reserves his most scathing epithets, calling them "vipers" and "snakes" (Matt. 23:33).

Though his ministry is one of compassion, Jesus is an agitator. His presence is polarizing, forcing people to take sides; there is no fence-sitting. He keeps doing things that startle even his most loyal devotees, like vandalizing the temple marketplace in broad daylight, during prime business hours (Matt. 21:12–13; Mark 11:15–17; Luke 19:45–46; John 2:14–16). And again, there's that thing he says about eating his flesh and drinking his blood (John 6:51–68).

Remember, we are reading the story two thousand years later, with the benefit of centuries of commentary, annotation, and explanation. But to truly understand the "loser" qualities of this self-proclaimed Messiah, put yourself in the context of ancient Palestine. All you know is, some no-name crackpot is running around the countryside, saying and doing the wildest things ever seen or heard. No wonder people called him insane or demon-possessed—not only, I think, to discredit and dismiss him, but also because he was healing the blind, the lame, and the lepers, and even raising the dead. To the average witness, Jesus easily could have been perceived as either a crafty con artist or a sorcerer.

So people said he was mad because of his crazy teachings, his claims of deity, and his miracles, which they considered to be some kind of trickery. But he did something else that, if he wasn't God, surely made him certifiably insane: when it became obvious that continuing such controversial activity was going to get him killed, he didn't tone it down. Instead, he escalated it—insulting the highest religious leaders, casting the money changers out of the temple, and continuing to insist that he was God.

If someone is running around making wild claims, fine. But if it becomes clear he is going to be executed for making them and he keeps making them anyway—now that's crazy. No one—absolutely *no one*—in his right mind would insist on standing by a self-perpetuated lie that would get him killed. Any sane person would recant the lie to save his life.

If it was a lie, that is.

But Jesus wasn't lying.

I think I understand why Jesus met such violent opposition from the religious leaders of his day. To measure spirituality, they had created a maze of stringent requirements by which they declared themselves "spiritual" and everyone else "sinners"—even though, in honesty, neither group could keep the impossible rules they had set up.

So Jesus, seeing their hypocrisy and the suffering it inflicted on their followers, called them on it. He told the truth and never backed down.

And he ended up with a bull's-eye burned into his chest.

Face it: If you were sitting in your comfortable pew in a suburban megachurch one Sunday morning, and your professionally-produced worship service was disrupted by a man of humble means, overturning the book tables, CD racks, and mocha counters in your foyer and shouting, "My house shall be called a house of prayer; but you are making it a den of robbers" (Matt. 21:13), you might get angry. You might even whip out your cell phone and call the police.

If the guy continued to disrupt, anger, and offend established churches everywhere, especially over a period of several years, it's likely there might be an outcry for his arrest.

And if he wouldn't relent and threatened to bring down an entire system that offered you, personally, a position of comfort and privilege, you might even want him dead.

That was the position of the Jewish religious leaders and Pharisees. They had waited so long for the Messiah, but they didn't understand him when he came.

The Anointed One, who had entered the world surrounded by rejection and scandal, was preparing to leave it the same way.

The disciples, however, were a different story. While the Jewish religious leaders grew more and more antagonistic, believing Jesus to be a charlatan or worse, these twelve men had spent three years completely sold out, believing Jesus to be the long-awaited Messiah. And he did seem to fulfill that role—in so many ways.

Except for that gory ending.

On the day Jesus was sentenced to die, I wonder what chaos took place among the disciples. I can only imagine their hushed conversations as they hid away in terror.

Why was God hanging on a cross—an execution method reserved for traitors and criminals, and the worst of them at that? It was bad enough for Jesus to be brought up on charges, but to be executed as a criminal among criminals, the worst of the worst, was a nightmare. For his followers, their entire belief system was collapsing around them. Their Lord—the one who had brought them hope, fulfillment, meaning, and purpose—had now been convicted of capital offenses and exposed (so it seemed) as a fraud. All the life-changing teachings and wondrous miracles of the past three years dissolved before their eyes.

I wonder if they felt that Jesus had duped them, betrayed them, taken them for a ride. I wonder if some of them spent that awful day remembering the previous three years, trying to discover any red flags they might have missed that pointed to Jesus being a fraud, just another self-proclaimed messiah in a sea of self-proclaimed messiahs. Scripture tells us they felt fear (John 20:19), but did they also feel more than a little stupid? Hoodwinked by a master deceiver, now nailed to a cross between two other low-life criminals?

The threat of danger and rejection that had shadowed Jesus from birth was now snuffing out his breath, crushing his new kingdom, and annihilating the dreams of all who had followed him.

And this scandalous end to Jesus's life raised issues for the new faith he left behind. Why base a religion on the teachings of someone who was a lunatic by all appearances and a criminal by verdict? After all, Jesus insisted on maintaining his wild teachings even as he saw they were sure to get him killed. And, as the crucifixion crowd so mockingly suggested (Mark 15:29–32; Luke 23:35–36), if he really was God, why not save himself? Didn't his failure to do so prove that he was a fraud?

And where was God in all of this? If Jesus was truly God's Son, why would God stand back and do nothing as Jesus was humiliated, tortured, and crucified? Even if all of this was for some greater purpose, wouldn't it still be a form of child sacrifice? Wasn't that forbidden by the law and the prophets (Deut. 12:31; Jer. 7:30–31; Mic. 6:7)? Surely there had to be another way.

After all, God is God. Couldn't he come up with a method of redemption that didn't involve spilled blood?

Two thousand years later, the scandal of Jesus's crucifixion continues to haunt religious thinkers. Recently I was listening to some talk show on the radio, and a caller described the story of Jesus's crucifixion as "sadomasochistic torture porn."

Obviously, the caller was a big fan.

But upon reflection, I thought: He's right. We Christ-followers commemorate and even celebrate the grisly torture and execution of an innocent human being. We re-create it in paintings, photographs, films, tapestries, and all kinds of other artistic expressions, down to the shredded flesh and gushing blood.

This Jesus was born rejected, lived rejected, and died rejected.

Yes, there can be no doubt. The Son of God was ... a loser.

During his entire ministry, he associated with losers. He attracted mostly the poor and low-born (1 Cor. 1:26). He befriended the sinful and corrupt, like Matthew and Zaccheus (Matt. 9:9–13; Luke 19:1–9). He touched the untouchables, like the woman of ill repute who washed his feet with perfume (Luke 7:36–50) and the woman who was unclean because of her bleeding (Mark 5:25–34). And two of his greatest evangelists—the woman at the well and Mary Magdalene—were, respectively, promiscuous (John 4:7–42) and demon-possessed (Luke 8:2; John 20:18).

Jesus upset the norms, introducing an upside-down reality: to live, you must die; to lead, you must serve; to win, you must lose it all. The Jewish masses expected their Messiah to gallop into Jerusalem on a white horse, crushing the long arm of the Roman Empire and booting the hated oppressors back to Rome with their tails between their legs. Instead, they got a carpenter—one who taught an obscure interpretation of the kingdom of God. He proclaimed the meek to be blessed and the last to be first. He knelt before his disciples and performed the filthiest act of service by washing their feet.

In truth, Jesus identified more with the "losers" of society than with the "winners." He did nothing to affirm the spiritual superiority of the religious leaders—the very ones who had the position to lend official legitimacy to his teachings. Instead, he preferred the company of those they called "sinners"—those who broke the religious leaders' own petty man-made laws.

Yes, Jesus chose to hang out with the outcasts and rejects.

And in choosing to be with them, he became one of them.

This is what makes Jesus's life and teaching so unique. Jesus was a loser not by default but by intention. Though he was in "very nature God," he "made himself nothing" (Phil. 2:6–7). He had more knowledge, power, and charisma than anyone else who ever lived, and he had everyone's attention. When it came to public acclaim, he could have climbed that ladder, jumped into that spotlight, grabbed that brass ring. He wasn't born a loser; he became one by choice.

This is a great mystery to me. Why? Why didn't he choose a life of fame and privilege? Surely he could have reached a wider audience from such a platform. So why did he choose instead to be identified with the lowliest?

The answer takes me back to my discussion of political rhetoric in the introduction of this chapter: I believe it is because humanity as a whole is a group that just doesn't have its act together.

We are all losers, fallen and broken and in need of a Savior. And it is with losers that Jesus chose to identify because they (we) make up humanity's largest demographic: one hundred percent. No one who ever lived—past, present, or future—has ever been anything else.

If Jesus had come any other way, the world would have missed the point. If he had lived a life of celebrity and privilege, he would have been distant, out of reach. There would have been a built-in disconnect between the lover and his beloved, the shepherd and his sheep. His teachings would be just empty words. After all, how could the masses ever connect with such teachings as "Blessed are the poor in spirit," "If anyone slaps you on the right cheek, turn to them the

other cheek also," or "Love your enemies and pray for those who persecute you" (Matt. 5:3, 39, 44) spoken from *inside* the palace walls?
To the rest of us poor slobs *outside* the palace, struggling through
day-to-day life, those statements would ring hollow, like edicts from
a holier-than-thou elitist with no clue of the suffering and injustice
of real life.

To be truly heard by the masses, Jesus had to insert himself into
the gritty context of human life. He had to become one of us. He
had to become a loser.

When disgusted religious leaders asked Jesus why he was associ-
ating with (read: contaminating himself by hanging around) partiers,
prostitutes, and tax cheats, Jesus stated flatly, "It is not the healthy
who need a doctor, but the sick" (Matt. 9:12).

Throughout this study, I have compared my life to each of the
twelve disciples to find commonality. And from the beginning I
have easily identified my sins and weaknesses with theirs. Yet it now
occurs to me that of all the losers discussed, Jesus is the only loser
who is actually trying to identify with ... *me*.

This is a remarkable act of grace. What is so special about my
broken-down soul, with all its faults and sins, that Jesus actually
wants to stand side by side with *me*—a proven failure? Even when
I push him away, even when I fall into yet another sin, he *chooses* to
step into my story.

Perhaps even more remarkable is this: Although I often feel (or
feign) shock and horror when I see a leader, a loved one, or even
myself commit the same screwups for the umpteenth time, Jesus is
never surprised at such failures. In fact, he expects them.

We put on masks—in public or even in private relationships—
to try to hide who we really are. Our greatest fear is that the worst of

what's inside us might leak out. We are ashamed, embarrassed by the cracks in our lives—and in truth, we should be. Our lives are a mess. If we're honest, we can see it each time we look in the mirror. We try to hide this truth from others, and even (as if we could) from God.

For most of my life as a Christ-follower, I have masked myself to try to hide from both God and others. For many years, I actually convinced myself that it worked.

It took a great implosion to shatter my illusion of a small God who is easily fooled by my feeble attempts to hide my real self. This implosion not only collapsed my framework of God but also blew the mask off of my head. I was naked—my embarrassment and shame exposed for all to see. But over time I have discovered that, despite my enormous discomfort, this exposure is just what Jesus wants. My pathetic mask was standing in the way of true relationship with him.

By choosing to identify with my brokenness, Jesus steps into my life with the full knowledge of who I am. He is not surprised by my faults, my sins, my selfishness. Like he has with every other loser since the dawn of time, Jesus knows exactly how to connect with me.

To identify with us losers, he lived as a loser.

His mission of making disciples out of losers was so important to him that he chose to become a loser himself. And that is why the King of kings is, ironically, the greatest loser of all.

14

THE KINGDOM OF LOSERS LIKE US

WHERE DO WE GO FROM HERE?

As I wrap up my personal exploration of the lives of Jesus's disciples, I have a confession to make.

First, the recap: I started this project shortly after receiving a powerful one-two punch that sent me sprawling onto the canvas. The first punch was when I went "all in" on an academic career, and walked away with nothing. The second was when I came home and lost the full-time teaching position I loved. Within six weeks of each other. In a recession.

And now, the confession: At the time of this writing, several years have passed, and I have to admit that no visible redemption has happened since then. No miracle has fallen from heaven; no act of mercy has appeared on my doorstep to tie everything together and infuse it all with meaning. There has been no "aha!"

moment of perspective, allowing me to see the bigger picture and all the good things that have come out of this disaster.

Nothing can be done about the doctoral program. The only remaining hard copy of my dissertation was such a painful reminder that I threw it away.

And my teaching career? I still consider teaching to be my desire and my calling, and I still look for opportunities to engage in it. But I still don't have the credentials increasingly sought by most high schools (a master's in teaching) or colleges (a PhD) and, due to debts already incurred, I truly do not have the reserves to keep paying for more education. So, except for the adjunct classes that I am able to get—and, to be honest, those come and go—I am still basically unemployed.

Through this crisis, I have learned that it is pointless to ask "why?" because no one can answer that question. So the question I'm working on instead is "what now?" I still live in a context of loss; I'm still trying to figure out the next steps. I continue to apply for all types of work—yet I am still unsure how to get out of this rut, even when I want to.

Perhaps even more frustrating is the suspicion that *I* haven't changed. As far as I can tell, despite much seeking through prayer and study, I have not grown since the disaster—at least, not in ways that are visible to me. I certainly don't feel any more spiritual than before; in fact, some days I feel less. I still have days when I struggle even to leave home and engage in the world.

Paul says that "suffering produces perseverance; perseverance, character; and character, hope" (Romans 5:3–4). So ... shouldn't this suffering purify me and make me a better person? Shouldn't I be Super-Christian by now, able to leap tall steeples with a single bound while deflecting Satan's arrows off my chest?

But no. Instead, like Job, I have sat by the garbage heap, licked my wounds, and sulked. Like Job, I have demanded an audience with God. Like Job, I have longed for justice. I have had to accept my losses, but I have earnestly desired relief from the overwhelming pain and confusion they have caused.

In fact, to numb the pain, I think there have been times when I overdosed on self-pity, like a drug: the more I consumed, the more I wanted. Wallowing in it felt better than moving on—something I didn't know how to do.

And I've barely mentioned my ongoing bouts of depression, anxiety, and bitterness (I can think of a million reasons not to forgive, none of which can slide past Jesus's unbending requirement to do so in Matthew 18:21–35), or the fact that I have to fight envy and despair whenever I hear of others starting or finishing their doctoral work. In my worst moments, I have even caught myself secretly wishing they might fail too—just to know the pain I feel.

Now that's a loser for you.

So I continue to wrestle with myself: my spirit knows I must seek God's perspective, pursue God's ways—but my flesh stubbornly demands justice, vengeance, sympathy. Often, my flesh seems to win. If I were to say I have experienced victory during this ordeal, I would be lying.

I realize, of course, that such a confession is likely to have two effects.

First, it may disqualify me from some spiritual "Hall of Faith," such as the one described in Hebrews 11.

Second, it may disappoint readers who were hoping for a book of answers on how to overcome "loserness," meaning how to move from loserdom to non-loserdom, because I don't have those answers;

I have not yet overcome. I was a loser when I started writing this book, and I am still a loser as I finish it.

Further, I believe that if I had somehow become a winner, shedding my loser identity and coming out on top, then I would be just another success story, with nothing to say to those who haven't "made it." Those who still feel like losers. Those who still *are* losers. Like me.

And you. If you're old enough to read a book like this, I am sure that you have experienced your share of loss and failure; you're a loser too.

And it is precisely because we are losers that we have something in common with the losers I've focused on in this book—the twelve disciples. From the bigot to the betrayer to the screwup, the disciples are all horribly broken, shockingly sinful, and desperately in need of a Savior.

They are losers like us.

Which makes them, and us, ideal candidates for redemption. And for kingdom work.

In fact, if Jesus were selecting his twelve disciples today, he might even choose you and me to be among them—as we are right now, in all our brokenness—with no requirements at all for status, success, or spiritual maturity (or lack thereof).

For me, this has been an important discovery.

It's not a new one: the flaws of all the "heroes of faith" are splattered throughout the Old and New Testaments, and often mentioned in sermon illustrations and Bible studies. But to me their lives always seemed detached and dead—like mere stories in a book—until I studied them in a way that was not objective and scientific but subjective and personal, and began to see them as flesh-and-blood humans who lived and struggled exactly as I do. Never again can I judge them as silly weaklings. No, I am one of them, hanging on by my last toenail to the fact that because Jesus chose them to follow him, there is great hope for the rest of us.

The body of Christ doesn't need more "experts" telling us all that's wrong with us and all that we should be doing to fix ourselves. No, it needs more losers—people who finally understand that the *only* thing they have going for them is that Jesus loves them.

Losers have, well, nothing to lose. They've already lost it. There's no one to impress. They're beyond thinking they have something to prove.

True losers can be many ugly things, but one thing they seldom are is hypocrites; and, as mentioned earlier, Jesus came down harder on hypocrites than on anyone else.

I believe this is why Jesus chose losers, rather than those at the "top of the heap," to be his disciples. He was setting the standard for the rest of the church, down through history. Because what he desires most is for his people—all of us—to become brutally honest about how small and needy we really are.

Look at this New Testament list of requirements for overseers and deacons in the church:

> Here is a trustworthy saying: Whoever aspires to be an overseer desires a noble task. Now the overseer is to be above reproach, faithful to his wife, temperate, self-controlled, respectable, hospitable, able to teach, not given to drunkenness, not violent but gentle, not quarrelsome, not a lover of money. He must manage his own family well and see that his

children obey him, and he must do so in a manner worthy of full respect. (If anyone does not know how to manage his own family, how can he take care of God's church?) He must not be a recent convert, or he may become conceited and fall under the same judgment as the devil. He must also have a good reputation with outsiders, so that he will not fall into disgrace and into the devil's trap.

In the same way, deacons are to be worthy of respect, sincere, not indulging in much wine, and not pursuing dishonest gain. They must keep hold of the deep truths of the faith with a clear conscience. They must first be tested; and then if there is nothing against them, let them serve as deacons. (1 Tim. 3:1–10)

In this list of qualifications for leadership in the church, two things stand out to me.

First, notice what *is* on the list. The qualifications are simply basic character requirements—pretty much the same requirements listed throughout Scripture for *all* believers. So, if all Christians are expected to exhibit these qualities, then all Christians who *do* exhibit them are qualified to be leaders in the church. Such positions are not for just a few elite candidates, but for any Christ-follower whose character fulfills the list.

Second, notice what is *not* on the list. There is no mention of such human credentials as achievement, education, or experience. There is no mention of impressive recommendations from big-name spiritual leaders of that time, or advanced degrees from the most prestigious schools of the day. Instead, the qualifications for ministry are based solely on God's work in a person's life.

Where we see a lack of experience and polish, God sees leadership potential.

Similarly, human credentials were notably lacking in the twelve losers on whom Jesus built his church. What made them world-changers was not their credentials, but simply their willingness to follow him.

They followed awkwardly.

They tripped and fell.

They had no idea what the heck Jesus was talking about.

But despite all their missteps, they followed him to his death, and ultimately to their own.

Tradition says that of the twelve original disciples, only one—John—died a natural death, and even he suffered persecution (he may have survived being poisoned[1] and being boiled in a cauldron[2]). As for the rest, Judas Iscariot committed suicide and the others were martyred for following Christ. Were it not for these twelve losers, the gospel message never would have spread beyond Jerusalem.

Exactly how the disciples lived and died is a subject widely debated by historians. However, as retold by tradition and various sources, especially the well-known *Foxe's Book of Martyrs*, their stories may have ended as described below.

- James the Less may have preached in Egypt and Israel and then been crucified.[3] However, some accounts say he survived being thrown from a tower, clubbed, and stoned, and then later died from being sawed into pieces.[4]

- Judas Thaddaeus may have been killed with arrows in Mesopotamia.[5]
- Simon the Zealot, according to Foxe, preached in Africa and Britain before being crucified,[6] although some accounts say he was killed by a mob in Persia.[7]
- Andrew preached in multiple areas, including Sebastopolis (later inhabited by the Ethiopians), and eventually was killed because he boldly opposed idol worship to the highest authorities. Like his brother Simon Peter, Andrew felt unworthy to be crucified in the same manner as his Lord; so he was crucified on an X-shaped cross (a type of cross now called "Andrew's Cross" in his honor) by a local governor in Greece.[8] He faced his own execution with unflinching courage, joy, and eagerness.[9]
- Nathanael (Bartholomew) translated the gospel of Matthew into the language of India and preached there, after which he was crucified, excoriated, and beheaded in Armenia.[10]
- Philip proclaimed salvation among the "barbarous nations" and was crucified and stoned in Phrygia.[11]
- Matthew (Levi) evangelized in Ethiopia and Egypt before being run through with a spear.[12]
- Thomas preached to the Medes and Persians before being slain in India by a lance[13] or a dart.[14]
- James, son of Zebedee and "son of thunder," traveled all around the Mediterranean and took up

residence in Spain, where he founded a number of churches.[15] He was killed by Herod (Acts 12:1–2), making him the second person after Stephen, and the first of the twelve disciples, reported to have been martyred for Christ. According to tradition, James's testimony was so powerful that one of his chief accusers became a Christian and was beheaded along with him, in AD 36.[16]

- James's brother John, the other "son of thunder," evangelized throughout Asia Minor and was exiled by Emperor Domitian to the island of Patmos. He wrote five New Testament books (John, 1 John, 2 John, 3 John, Revelation) and apparently was allowed to return to Ephesus before he died in about AD 100, in his nineties—the last of the disciples to die.[17]

- Simon Peter evangelized throughout Asia Minor and Rome,[18] where he was crucified. He is said to have been crucified upside down, at his own request, because he felt unworthy to die in the same position as his Lord.[19]

Much of this information is based on tradition, so scholars may debate the details. And that's okay. That debate is for other venues.

The point is this: Jesus handpicked a group of total losers to be his disciples, and for three years they did nothing but whine, bicker, and squabble, striving pathetically (and futilely) to become winners.

Then Jesus died and rose again.

That single event made the difference. After that, the disciples finally understood that the whole human story isn't about us; it's about Christ. Once they grasped this, they spread the news with such passion that they were willing to give their lives for him, and for those he came to save. And their witness continues today, two millennia after their deaths.

Such is the transforming power of accepting our loserness and acknowledging God as the true winner, the star of the story, the Lord of all.

Jesus himself showed us how to lose everything and give God his rightful place. In the garden, just before his crucifixion, Jesus prayed, "Father, if you are willing, take this cup from me; yet not my will, but yours be done" (Luke 22:41–42).

Since Jesus's resurrection, many losers—including the disciples—have lost everything, even their lives, for their faith in him. But their losses give off a sweet aroma that lingers throughout history. These losers could not know the impact they made in their brief time on earth. They simply surrendered to God's will.

So why has Jesus always, then and now, chosen losers to lead the kingdom?

I think there are four main reasons, all closely related: teachableness, lack of ego, brokenness, and empathy. These are the areas in which losers truly excel.

First, losers are teachable. If you already know everything, then what could Jesus possibly do with you—or for you? Is there anything he could teach you?

As a doctoral candidate at a respected British university, I was sometimes tempted to think I didn't need to be taught—or worse, corrected—by those with lesser degrees. And I looked forward to having more education than anyone else in my workplace.

But that smugness came between me and God.

All my life I felt at a disadvantage. I actually believed that, in order to be on a level playing field with others, I had to one-up them. So I pushed myself academically. And somewhere in my journey, I think I started to believe that the world's most highly educated people were a sort of presidential cabinet for God. I think I imagined that as soon as I had my PhD, God was going to come to me and ask, "Dan, what do you think I should do now?"

How insane is that?

But the moment my oral defense imploded, my position plummeted from that of a PhD candidate, with all of the opportunities and the bright future associated with it, to that of a helpless, stupefied reject. And believe me, the distance between those two poles is a breathtaking drop. It didn't kill me physically, but honestly there were times when I wished it had.

The result was that my life became trapped in a rut of self-loathing and grief. Especially at first, the only relief seemed to be oceans of sympathy—from myself and others.

Over time I grew tired of this rut, but I could not find a way out. In many ways, I still haven't. I still have no secure career path, no dream, no future.

But it is precisely at this point that the loser is completely open to suggestions. Is the answer to wait in silence for God? Do I need to rely on my spiritual community to help lift me out if they can, or at least support me through my darkness? How can I see this event through eternal eyes? Is my flesh overpowering my spirit as I self-medicate with pity, bitterness, and unforgiveness?

How do I get past this roadblock, this impossible wall that I can't get over, under, around, or through?

Losers know that God doesn't answer to them. They know they'll never figure it out, and they have given up trying. They are powerless. They have no choice but to learn from God.

So they wait. And listen.

And at some point during their waiting, a step of grace appears at the base of the impassable wall.

After several years in my rut, one New Year's Eve I made a resolution. I resolved that in the upcoming year, I would echo Jesus's prayer before his crucifixion. First, he made his request to God: "If you are willing, take this cup from me." Then he ended with a prayer of utter submission: "Yet not my will, but yours be done" (Luke 22:42).

Short and simple. But not easy. I knew I had already made my request to God (for a job, a career, a future), so all that remained was to pray the rest of the prayer: "Not my will, but yours be done."

Within days, I caught myself adding qualifiers: "Your will be done—but I would really appreciate it if…" or "Your will be done … but could you please…?" I found it surprisingly hard to repeat Jesus's prayer with nothing added, and even harder to mean it.

However, I can honestly say that the longer I've lived in my prison of inescapable pain, the more willing I've become to learn how to pray the prayer, "Not my will, but yours," if only because I have no other choice left.

That point brings me to the second reason Jesus picks losers: lack of ego.

Losers are egoless, in the sense that they are no longer striving to build an "empire of the self." They have stopped chasing things like identity, image, status, and position.

When a person has an image to protect, much attention is devoted to building and maintaining it. Celebrities and politicians hire publicists to do this work on their behalf, but the truth is, we all try to protect our image. And the more time and energy we devote to this pursuit, the less we have for authentic kingdom work.

Even Christians may cultivate an image that projects deep spirituality, advanced biblical or theological knowledge, admirable self-denial, or great concern for social justice. But what if, instead of trying to merely *project* those qualities, we all sought God's help to actually *develop* them?

To a loser, ego no longer matters. A loser is a loser because he has failed. A loser is a loser because she has been spit out, discarded, abandoned. All image seeking is over. Losers are left standing in their own flabby nakedness, having nothing to offer the world. Yet it is only when we are stripped to this humiliating nakedness that Jesus begins to clothe us with something beautiful and amazing.

James and John started out as the bickering, self-seeking sons of thunder; but by the end of their lives, James was so meek and Christlike that even his enemies were converted, and John was so selfless and compassionate that he became known as "the disciple of love."

At some point, after the cross, they finally started loving Jesus more than they loved themselves.

That's a radical change.

After losing my PhD and my career, my identity vanished. I dreaded the question, "So what do you do?" I had nothing to say. People are kind and sympathetic, but that doesn't necessarily mean they want to hire you.

So, to pull myself out of my abyss of self-pity, I climbed up on that step of grace at the base of my unscalable wall. Since I couldn't find anyone to pay me for my experience and abilities, I decided to give them away freely by volunteering at my church. I, a person with a bachelor's degree, a master's degree, and seven years of doctoral training behind me, am now serving as ... a receptionist.

I answer phones, buzz people through the front door, and do other odd jobs. And believe it or not, sometimes I fail at even these small tasks. I've disconnected people, I've misrouted calls, and—on one especially frustrating day—I unknowingly punched a button which, instead of screening calls for the pastoral staff, forwarded those calls directly to them. I could hear the calls ringing through, but I couldn't intercept them—until someone finally figured it out.

Yes, it was embarrassing. The truth is, I'm not even great at entry-level work.

But surprisingly, I love it. I love just being around the business of the church, no matter how minor my role might be. For me, it's not about making sure that my unique talents are well utilized. It's not about ego. It's just about serving—giving my insignificant self to God to use as he chooses. (Remember my prayer: Not my will, but yours be done.) If God has something in mind later for using any of my other gifts, fine. I will cross that bridge when I get to it. For now, I am happy to serve the church by awkwardly answering phones.

In the old song "Jesus Loves Me," there's a line that says, "We are weak, but he is strong." But how can he be strong through our weakness when we are constantly trying to show the world how great we are?

And even if the world is presently impressed with us, just wait—there will come a time when it isn't. Each of us will spend at least part of our lives on the scrap heap. Everyone does.

Losers feel quite comfortable on that heap. Nothing else is left. And this is when redemption comes through.

Which brings me to the third reason Jesus chooses losers to do kingdom work: brokenness.

Losers, breakable and broken, are the perfect vessels through which God's glory can brightly shine.

The apostle Paul uses this metaphor of breakable vessels to describe God's people:

> For God, who said, "Let light shine out of darkness," made his light shine in our hearts to give us the light of the knowledge of God's glory displayed in the face of Christ. But we have this treasure in jars of clay to show that this all-surpassing power is from God and not from us. (2 Cor. 4:6–7)

In this metaphor, the treasure is kept not in a holy ark, or a golden temple, or a sacred tomb, but in fragile earthen vessels—jars of clay.

Now, that's definitely not the most secure choice for storing priceless treasure.

But this treasure is not meant to be stored. The jars must be broken and the treasure poured out by grace to the world.

I thought I had finished this breaking and pouring out process long ago. After growing up in a broken home, I went on to overcome the statistical pitfalls attached to children of divorce, including higher rates of suicide, substance abuse, and dropping out of school.[20] By the grace of God, I beat the odds. I finished high school, graduated from college, completed a master's degree, got married, and eventually found a career—teaching—that I really loved. I believed that experiencing all the pain of my parents' divorce was the breaking of the jar and that attaining an advanced degree and a career in academia would be the pouring out of God's grace.

But now I think this view is incomplete. I think the breaking of the jar and the pouring out of God's treasure happens not once, but perpetually. God is continually breaking the vessel, continually pouring out the treasure. To be honest, I still don't understand exactly how, but that doesn't mean it's not happening; it only means I can't see it. And when it hurts like crazy, I remind myself that pain can be for good, like an incision to remove a tumor.

It's almost as if God were saying, "Given your pain and struggles while growing up, the education you did achieve truly was an act of grace poured out on your life. But if you think *that* was amazing, just wait till you see how I can use you *without* a PhD."

Could it be that my particular treasure can be poured out only without that degree? After all, if my dissertation had passed, it probably would be sitting in a dusty library somewhere, unread and forgotten, just another number in an online catalog. How would *that* be an outpouring of God's grace?

But instead, I have a unique story—one that only a limited number of people can tell. After all, you're reading a whole book that came into being through unbearable pain and brokenness. Pain is inescapable; the heroes (uh, losers) in the Bible, including Jesus, weren't spared from pain, and we won't be either. But we must do what they did: we must climb up on that step of grace through faith and share our stories, especially the painful parts.

Remember, we are all part of a great story that is really about

God, not us. He is the number one character (read: winner), and we are all secondary (read: losers).

I first heard this idea in a sermon, and it greatly irritated me because, at least once in a while, *I* want to play the lead.

I keep fighting for a better part.

I keep trying to upstage God.

But losers are broken people who have come to submit to *God's* story, to acknowledge God's place at center stage and their own place at—well, wherever God wants. Losers understand their rightful place—and God's.

Yes, we are only supporters, bit players, extras in the story; but that doesn't mean we don't count. When the disciples shifted their perspective and stopped competing with God for center stage, they became powerful agents for spreading the new gospel to the whole world, ultimately affecting history far more than generals, kings, and emperors.

And that leaves the fourth reason Jesus prefers to use losers for kingdom work: empathy. Losers have it; others don't. Only losers, broken as they are, can speak to the pain and brokenness of other losers. They have earned that right.

Let's face it, when we experience pain, we don't need to be preached at by people who "have it all together." They may reach, but they just can't touch. In fact, they often do more harm than good by spouting pat answers or beating us over the head with Scripture verses, instead of just mourning with us. (One scripture that is often quoted abusively, in my opinion, to Christians experiencing great loss is Romans 8:28: "And we know that in all things God works for the good of those who love him, who have been called according to his purpose." I call such abuse "being Romans 8:28'ed to death.")

No, when we really hurt, we don't need platitudes. We need to hear from others who have also endured deep pain, who truly understand.

After the loss of my PhD, I occasionally heard some remarks that really hurt. One of them was, "Well, it's not the worst thing that can happen."

If you ever meet someone who has suffered a great loss, don't say that.

People who say such hurtful things may be speaking truth, but there's no understanding, no empathy. Unless they've been where I've been and felt what I've felt, their words sound hollow. Their smugness trivializes the event, causing even more pain.

And I've been on the other side too. When I taught high school, I'd often see a nervous job seeker sitting outside the headmaster's office, waiting for an interview. I'd smile and nod as I passed, but deep inside, I was thankful it wasn't me. I had a job.

Glad I'm not them, I thought.

Now I *am* "them." So now I truly am qualified to come alongside others who are where I've been. I *know.* I understand.

Jesus needs his followers to comprehend, on a deeply personal level, what it means to be broken. He came to reach losers; he commands his followers to do the same. People can never hear the gospel message if it is "spoken down" to them. They can only hear it from those who bear the scars of brokenness, healed by grace.

When I was in seminary, one of my professors received a heart transplant. During a chapel service, he told the story of two other heart transplant recipients: one who was preparing for a transplant, and another who already had been through it. At the first man's request, the second opened his shirt, bared his chest, and allowed the first man to run his fingers along the scar. The scar provided assurance that someone else had already gone through this terrifying experience, and had come out stronger, more healed, and more alive than ever.

A scar is a reminder of pain and suffering, but it is also a sign of hope and encouragement to others.

When Jesus prayerfully selected his disciples, he did not choose people overflowing with wealth, intellect, confidence, talent, or power. Instead, he chose twelve ordinary bumblers. His only requirement was that they follow him. As far as Jesus was concerned, these were the people with the greatest potential to manifest the kingdom of God on earth.

It is no different today.

I started this journey to see if I, as a loser, could be of any use in the kingdom of God. I held up each loser disciple to my face, like a mirror. And I saw myself in each of them.

They were not spiritual superstars. They were not the cream of the crop. They were broken, flawed, and sinful.

And, in a moment of overwhelming grace, a still, small voice inside me whispers that if Jesus used them anyway, then maybe he can use me—and you, too.

In the world's eyes, we are losers.

In Jesus's eyes, we are disciples.

And being in both categories, we are in good company.

NOTES

Chapter 1: An Introduction to Losers

1. The online quiz I took is no longer available, but there are many others. For example, try http://www.quizrocket.com/loser-geek-dork-nerd.

2. The reasons why my PhD could not be salvaged are a bit complex. My website, www.danielhochhalter.com, explains some of them.

3. I did have two advisors—one in England and one in the United States—but in this book, "my advisor" typically means the British one.

4. From http://www.gotoquiz.com/are_you_a_loser_30.

5. From http://wiki.answers.com/q/what_is_a_loser.

6. From http://answers.ask.com/Reference/Other/what_is_a_loser.

7. From http://www.urbandictionary.com/define.php?term=loser.

8. During the course of my youth ministry, I discovered three small books about the disciples: *The Twelve* by Leslie B. Flynn; *13 Men Who Changed the World* by H. S. Vigeveno; and *The Gospel According to Judas* by Ray S. Anderson. These works, which are primarily objective studies of the disciples, inspired me to begin my own more subjective journey, identifying with each disciple's story in a very personal way.

Chapter 4: The Shadow-Dweller

1. Quoted in Charles R. Swindoll, *Improving Your Serve* (Nashville: Thomas Nelson, 1984), 24.

Chapter 5: The Bigot

1. Merriam-Webster.com, s.v. "bigot," accessed July 12, 2014, http://www.merriam-webster.com/dictionary/bigot.

2. It should be noted that this disciple generally is called Bartholomew when the disciples are listed by roster (Matt. 10:3; Mark 3:18; Luke 6:14; Acts 1:13), but Nathanael virtually everywhere else.

Chapter 7: The Uber-Loser

1. Jon Trott and Mike Hertenstein, "Selling Satan: The Tragic History of Mike Warnke," *Cornerstone*, 21, issue no. 98 (July 1992). This extensive article, which investigated and refuted Warnke's claims through systematic research and multiple corroborating sources, was later expanded into a book, *Selling Satan: The Evangelical Media and the Mike Warnke Scandal*. The original article archive (http://www.cornerstonemag.com/features/iss098/warnke_index.htm) currently is inaccessible, but the article text is available at these locations: http://www.holysmoke.org/sdhok/warnke1.htm (with "Higher Education?" sidebar text) and http://web.archive.org/web/20110629063019/http://www.cornerstonemag.com/features/iss098/sellingsatan.htm (without "Higher Education?" sidebar text).

2. Trott and Hertenstein, "Selling Satan."

3. Trott and Hertenstein, "Selling Satan."

4. From July through November 1992, the *Lexington Herald-Leader* published at least seven articles (three on page A1) on the Warnke controversy. To view them, visit http://www.newslibrary.com (also called http://www.nl.newsbank.com) and use "Search Print Archives" to search for "Warnke."

Chapter 8: The Betrayer

1. Dorothy Sayers, *The Man Born to Be King* (San Francisco: Ignatius Press, 1990 [reprinted with permission; © 1943 by Dorothy L. Sayers]), 24.

2. The details of Judas's suicide are beyond the scope of this book. Matthew 27:3–10 says he hanged himself in a field bought by the chief priests; Acts 1:18 says he fell headlong, burst open, and spilled his intestines in a field he bought himself. Both agree that the field in which he died was purchased with the money paid to him for betraying Christ.

Chapter 9: The Doubter

1. C. S. Lewis, *A Grief Observed* (New York: Bantam Books, 1976), 35.

2. William Barclay, *The Gospel of John*, Vol. 2, The Daily Study Bible Series, rev. ed. (Philadelphia, PA: The Westminster Press, 1975), 277.

Chapter 10: The Egotist

1. With a few exceptions such as Luke 8:51 and 9:28, the Gospels consistently list James first, as in these passages: Matthew 4:21; 10:2, 17:1; Mark 1:19; 3:17; 5:37; 9:2; 10:35; 13:3; 14:33; Luke 5:10; 6:14.

2. Eugene H. Peterson, *The Message: The Bible in Contemporary Language* (Colorado Springs, CO: NavPress, 2002), Luke 9:5.

Chapter 11: The Kid

1. Paul Cartledge, *Thermopylae: The Battle That Changed the World* (New York: The Overlook Press, Peter Mayer Publishers, 2006), 80.

2. A. R. Colón with P. A. Colón, *A History of Children: A Socio-Cultural Survey Across Millennia* (Westport, CT: Greenwood Press, 2001), 91–92.

3. Arnold A. Dallimore, *George Whitefield: God's Anointed Servant in the Great Revival of the Eighteenth Century* (Wheaton, IL: Crossway Books, 1990), 24.

4. For a brief history of these students and how their passion started the Protestant missions movement, see the Williams College archives at http://archives.williams.edu/buildinghistories/missionpark/revival.html.

Chapter 12: The Screwup

1. Despite Peter's tremendous growth over time from fearful (Matt. 14:30; Mark 14:66–72; Gal. 2:11–12) to fearless (Acts 2:14–41; 4:8–17), he may have battled fear all his life, further proving that Jesus can do great things even with losers who never quite overcome their loser traits. Foxe (12-13) and others repeat the apocryphal story (Acts of Peter XXXV) that Peter, late in life, is fleeing Rome to avoid martyrdom when he has a vision of Jesus going the other way. Peter asks where he is going (in Latin, "*Quo vadis?*"), and Jesus replies that he is going to Rome to be crucified again. This exchange apparently convicts Peter and gives him the courage to share in Christ's sufferings, because he does return to Rome and eventually is crucified. Quoted in Bernhard Pick, *The Apocryphal Acts of Paul, Peter, John, Andrew, and Thomas* (Chicago: The Open Court Publishing Co., 1909; republished by Forgotten Books, 2012), 114–115.

Chapter 14: The Kingdom of Losers Like Us

1. Leslie B. Flynn, *The Twelve* (Wheaton, IL: Victor Books, 1982), 68.

2. Flynn, *The Twelve*, 22.

3. H. S. Vigeveno, *13 Men Who Changed the World* (Ventura, CA: Regal Books, 1966), 74.

4. Flynn, *The Twelve*, 22, 114.

5. Flynn, *The Twelve*, 22.

6. John Foxe, *Foxe's Book of Martyrs* (New Kensington, PA: Whitaker House, 1981), 6–7.

7. Flynn, *The Twelve*, 22, 127.

8. Flynn, *The Twelve*, 22, 44.

9. Foxe, *Foxe's Book of Martyrs*, 7–9. Foxe's detailed account tells how Andrew passionately embraced martyrdom for Christ, exclaiming in part upon seeing his own cross: "O cross, most welcome and long looked for! with a willing mind, joyfully and desirously, I come to thee, being the scholar of him which did hang on thee; because I have always been thy lover, and have coveted to embrace thee."

10. Foxe, *Foxe's Book of Martyrs*, 7.

11. Foxe, *Foxe's Book of Martyrs*, 9.

12. Foxe, *Foxe's Book of Martyrs*, 9.

13. Flynn, *The Twelve*, 22.

14. Foxe, *Foxe's Book of Martyrs*, 6.

15. Flynn, *The Twelve*, 55.

16. Foxe, *Foxe's Book of Martyrs*, 6. This account is also mentioned in Flynn, *The Twelve*, 54–55.

17. Flynn, *The Twelve*, 68–69.

18. Flynn, *The Twelve*, 34.

19. Foxe, *Foxe's Book of Martyrs*, 12–13. See the chapter on Peter for more on his fears, which he overcame when he submitted to martyrdom.

20. Patrick F. Fagan and Robert Rector, "The Effects of Divorce on America," The Heritage Foundation, June 5, 2000, http://www.heritage.org/research/reports/2000/06/the-effects-of-divorce -on-america/.

CPSIA information can be obtained at www.ICGtesting.com
Printed in the USA
BVOW01s1417090914

366105BV00004B/128/P